EATING NATURALLY

EATING NATURALLY
Recipes for food with fibre

Maggie Black *and* Pat Howard

FABER & FABER · London and Boston

First published in 1980
by Faber and Faber Limited
3 Queen Square London WC1N 3AU
Phototypeset by Western Printing Services Ltd, Bristol
Printed in Great Britain by
Redwood Burn Ltd, Trowbridge and Esher
All rights reserved

British Library Cataloguing in Publication Data

Black, Maggie
  Eating naturally
  1. Cookery (Natural foods)
  I. Title   II. Howard, Pat
  641.5'63   TX741

  ISBN 0-571-11602-7
  ISBN 0-571-11603-5 Pbk

For P. B. H.

Nor is this our cafe in our Liquors only, and in our gaieties of Drefs, but in almoft every thing elfe; particularly in our table Exceffes; the waft and wantonnefs in Eating is come to fuch a height, that it is the fupport of innumerable People: what a fwarm of Gardiners, Poulterers, Paftry-Cooks, Eating-houfes, &c. are fupported by the mere Extraordinaries of Eating; raifing Plants by mere Violence, and as it were a rape upon the Earth; forcing her to produce things before her time, and as it were in fpite of feafons, climates, forward or backward Springs, and the moft obftinate oppofition of natural Caufes?

What Rapes are committed upon nature in the production of Animals as well as Plants? making the Ewes bring Lambs all the Winter; fatting Calves to a monftrous fize, ufing cruelties and contrary diets to the poor Brute, to whiten its Flefh for the Palates of the Ladies, and to gorge the dainty Stomachs of thofe that lay up their felicity in Eating fine, as they call it?

DANIEL DEFOE
The Complete English Tradesman, vol. 2, 1721

CONTENTS

ACKNOWLEDGEMENTS

We, the authors, want, very much, to thank the many people who have patiently and generously given their time, skill and critical palates to testing, tasting and assessing the recipes in this book.

We would like to thank the following manufacturers and agencies who supplied products for testing our recipes: Edward Billington (Sugars) Ltd—for natural muscovado and demerara sugars; Farmhouse Bakery Products (Canterbury) Ltd—for Hoppers wholemeal pastry cases; Lotus Foods—for textured vegetable protein; Bernard Matthews Ltd—for Norfolk Turkey fillets; and the Swiss Cheese Union—for Swiss Gruyère cheese. We owe a particular debt to Allinson, whose stoneground 100% wholewheat flour was used for our wholemeal recipes, and who generously sponsored the cover photograph.

We would also like to thank the following who have given their own trusted recipes to the book: Elizabeth Lambert Ortiz, Patricia Jacobs, Barbara Morrison, Hilary Burns and Ann Mason. E. P. Publishing Ltd have kindly allowed us to use copyright recipes. Besides these, our thanks go to Ingrid Smith, who typed Part I no less than ten times; Marcelle Letacq, who corrected and typed all the recipes several times and who tested and tasted many of the dishes as well; and the publishers, who patiently waited for the manuscript, and never expressed the frustration they must have felt.

M.B.
P.H.

PART I · NATURAL EATING—WHOLE FOODS AND THEIR FIBRE

NATURAL EATING

The purpose of this book is twofold. First, we want to consider some of the effects which losses caused by modern food-processing can have on one's health. There has been a growing tendency in recent years to remove the fibre, along with impurities, from certain foods—this amounts to throwing the baby out with the bath water! Second, we want to show how the value of our meals can be improved in ways which are interesting as well as nutritious. We hope to demonstrate that the best way to nourish our bodies effectively is to eat 'naturally'. This means eating 'something of everything'—using natural food-products where possible without letting them become unnaturally important in our minds.

PROCESSED FOODS

Eating naturally means eating 'something of everything'. It also means using natural products whenever possible. It is more nutritious and more satisfying to eat a home-baked wholegrain or herb loaf than a commercially produced, ready-sliced alternative which is tasteless by comparison. Sometimes, though, it may be more convenient to buy the wrapped, sliced loaf. If this has to happen then it is vital that it should be just as safe to eat, if not always as wholesome, as the home-baked one.

Successive governments have been as concerned about the overall effects of 'processing' as about the additives which are put into our food. The outcome is that all processed food-products in the United Kingdom now have to conform to rigidly enforced legal standards for safety. Extensive research must be carried out to ensure that, as far as possible, the public is protected from any harmful side-effects which may result from the processing techniques.

Constant developments in food technology have resulted in an increasing number of 'convenience' products. It seems almost impossible for most of us to manage without many of them. How could the average flat-dweller grind his own corn, for instance?

Many valuable foods are only processed so that they take up less space than the equivalent fresh ones. Others are processed so that they can be kept for longer. This is really just a development of the time-honoured home-preserving done by our ancestors, except that the processing methods are usually safer and more assured. They are certainly useful. As a bonus, many products which are not readily available here can be imported as 'convenience' foods to give meals variety and interest.

Because of the benefits they can offer, we believe that processed foods (including the commercially preserved, easy-to-use products we call 'convenience' foods) should not be completely excluded from the store-cupboard. Most extensively processed and pre-packaged foods should, however, be used with discretion and generally in limited quantities compared with fresh foods. If these foods are used to the exclusion of fresh foods, many unpleasant results may occur. Large numbers of people do not enjoy the good health they should, partly at least because their lifestyle includes a faulty diet. It is now thought that long-term ill-effects can result from eating large amounts of refined foods at the expense of other, more natural, products.

Any food which can contribute to a balanced diet promotes good health—provided that not too much of it is eaten. This means that almost any food eaten in moderation is a 'health' food. It is just as important to maintain the natural *balance* of nutrients in the body as it is to get enough of each individual nutrient. If you eat sensibly, there should be no need to take any vitamin or mineral supplements unless they have been medically prescribed.

NON-REFINED FOODS

Why do we feel the need to write a recipe book if we are only advocating 'normal and natural' eating? Won't an ordinary general recipe book do? The answer is 'no'—unless you already know how to amend and interpret ingredients and suggestions. If you cannot do this, you will just perpetuate the imbalance which exists in many modern diets.

We believe that our book will help you to eat naturally balanced meals by giving you the chance to make sure that at least one meal a day contains some of the non-refined products which have the most nutritional value. The types of food to choose should be obvious if we explain the difference between the various groups of non-refined or 'health' foods.

ORGANICALLY GROWN FOODS

These are plant and animal foods grown or reared without artificially manufactured chemicals or fertilizers, and processed without artificial additives. Many people cannot afford such produce and do not have the time to buy and process it as often as they should, so that it can be used in peak condition. This means that its benefits are restricted and often lost. It must therefore be acknowledged that certain artificial additives are of immense benefit in helping to overcome the problem of keeping food fresh. The addition of minute quantities of preservative to some foods, for instance certain fruit and vegetables, does mean that they can be eaten with safety everywhere instead of being consumed only where they are grown.

WHOLE FOODS

These are the ones from which the natural fibre has not been removed. The everyday foods most affected by the removal of natural fibre are breads, pasta, rice and breakfast cereals. White flour makes lighter, larger, baked goods than wholemeal flour, which look more pleasant. For this reason, it has been popular for many centuries. Similarly, many people think that white rice looks more attractive than the more nourishing brown rice. The process of removing the fibre (and other impurities) and improving the colour of foods is called refining.

Wheat is the most familiar cereal in the Western world. A wheat grain has three main parts: the outer husk, or bran; the wheat germ; and the starchy endosperm, or store. The wheat germ is where the grain's minerals and vitamins are found and is a good source of them. Flour is produced from the endosperm. Most household white flour is of about 70% extraction rate. This means that 30% of the original whole wheat, most of which is husk, has been removed during processing. Although the law requires that some minerals and vitamins are returned to the refined flour, none of the husk is replaced. A similar process occurs during rice production but there are no legal requirements for 'revitalization'.

Recent scientific discoveries seem to show that the husk is much more valuable than we used to think. Publicity concerning this loss of husk has now led to a big demand for 'low extraction' flours and other unrefined cereals. As a result they are now fairly easy to obtain. (81% extraction flour, which we have used in a lot of our recipes, is available in most supermarkets.)

Thus, a 'whole food' is one from which nothing has been removed. This means that, besides its complete vital vitamin and mineral content, it also contains a significantly larger amount of the substance we call 'fibre'.

FIBRE

Doctors now suspect that the decreased fibre intake of the last fifty years or so in Western society may be responsible for certain modern, quite specific, physical ailments. Studying the diet of groups of peoples is part of the work of an epidemiologist. In recent years, fibre has come under scrutiny by these specialist scientists, and a number of carefully conducted studies have taken place, particularly in rural areas of Africa.

Like many surveys which lead to new discoveries, these studies started from small beginnings. Doctors noticed that many disorders which are common in the Western world hardly occurred at all in the African bush communities. These included constipation, piles, varicose veins and diverticular disease of the colon.* It was not long before the diets of each group were broadly assessed. It was noted that the main difference between the two groups was the amount of fibre they ate. The rural African does not have access to modern processing plants and his intake of fruit and vegetables is generally larger than that of his Western counterpart.

This was a very important discovery. It was found that certain disorders could be treated comparatively cheaply by modifying the fibre intake. It also meant that these disorders could, possibly, be prevented in the first place if the fibre intake was adjusted early enough.

The initial surveys have subsequently been extended. As a result, doctors have confirmed that many common disorders of the lower digestive tract, in particular, can be eliminated or at least alleviated by the inclusion of an adequate amount of fibre in the diet. It is also possible that the way the body uses fats may be affected, and some kinds of heart disease may be aggravated by a fibre-deficient diet. This is an impressive list of possibilities. Should we not, then, top up our fibre intake, if only to be on the safe side?

* Diverticular disease is the appearance of balloon-like pockets in the lower intestinal wall. These are caused by the increased pressure which occurs when there is a consistent effort to pass hard stools. Bacteria can collect and multiply in these pockets causing a local inflammation or diverticulitis.

WHAT IS FIBRE?

Basically, fibre is the 'wood husk' structure of plants, consisting mainly of cellulose, which is a material not absorbed by the digestive system. Most fibre consists of structures of complex carbohydrate molecules which are largely resistant to digestion. There is another category of fibre called lignin which is not a carbohydrate. In its natural state it is largely reponsible for the quality of 'woodiness' which occurs in certain plant structures. Lignin is extremely resistant to digestion.

Fibre forms part of a great many but not all foods. It is largely found in wholegrain cereals and products containing them, fruits, vegetables and nuts. On page 142, you will find a list of the fibre content of a range of commonly used foods. Other important foods contain little or no fibre, but to eat 'naturally' we must include them in our meals because they contain valuable nutrients. Perhaps the best example is milk which contains no fibre at all but is an excellent source of calcium and protein. Page 142 gives you the major sources of the most important nutrients.

HOW DOES FIBRE 'WORK' IN OUR BODIES?

We have said that fibre is essentially composed of cellulose. This has a complex chemical structure which allows it to absorb a lot of water and become 'bulky'. Think how rice absorbs water during cooking, and swells.

After eating a meal, enzymes are activated in the bowel or gut. These are able to break the food down into basic proteins, fats and carbohydrates. In other words, the food is digested. The digested nutrients are then absorbed from the gut into the bloodstream so that they can be used by the body. This is the natural way a normal healthy person obtains his nourishment. Not the entire bulk of the food is absorbed, however. Much waste material is formed which must be cleared from the gut, otherwise the digestive system will become clogged. Before long, this will cause constipation and illness.

Fibre remains virtually unchanged as it passes through the gut. It forms the bulk of the material which is not absorbed by the body. This is propelled forward along the lower gut by a chain-like series of squeezing and relaxing actions by the muscles of the gut-wall. Then, like the waste material, it is excreted as stools. This is where fibre is important. It adds bulk to the stools because its structure enables it to absorb a lot of water which is present in the lower gut. This helps to create large, soft and well-formed stools. It follows that a lack of fibre in food leads to the passage of small, dry, hard stools which are difficult and possibly painful to pass. This can give rise to unpleasant conditions such as chronic constipation and haemorrhoids. Rather than take to artificial laxatives as a cure, it seems simpler and more natural to ensure that plenty of fibre is eaten in the first place.

So much for constipation. What about the other ailments we have mentioned? The most dramatic and serious illnesses of which fibre is said to reduce the risk are cancer of the colon and some types of heart disease. Every normal healthy body makes certain substances which can sometimes become poisonous and dangerous. These accumulate in the bowel and are generally eliminated in the stools. However, a chronically constipated person cannot get rid of them. It is now thought that such an increase in poisons in the system may lead to more serious physical complications, including cancer and heart disease. So far the evidence for this is still largely circumstantial. However, it is yet another reason, if one is needed, for making sure that one's bowels function well and smoothly rather than sluggishly and ineffectively.

An answer often gives rise to more questions. How much fibre do we need to help us maintain a smooth, regular bowel function? We must return to our first suggestion that sensible eating means, first and foremost, eating a little of everything. This is as true of fibre as of anything else. Overdoses of fibre will not provide a near-miracle cure for any of the diseases that we have mentioned. In fact some doctors feel that too *much* fibre may prevent or delay the absorption of certain essential minerals and other nutrients into the bloodstream.

It is wise to choose natural rather than artificially isolated sources of fibre. These natural foods are fruits, vegetables, unrefined cereals and nuts. Eating them provides excellent, natural tasty meals without recourse to any additives at all, even such natural ones as bran! We have chosen recipes containing them, and we hope these will attract you and encourage you to use them more. These dishes will increase your fibre intake naturally by using widely varied foods (sometimes including processed ones) which your family, friends and you yourself will enjoy.

It is hard to assess what anyone's ideal of intake of fibre should be; everyone's need is different. The best way to find out your own 'ideal level' is to increase your intake gradually until you feel that your bowels are working really effectively. You can do this by including just one high-fibre recipe each day to begin with. This can then be increased until you feel that you have reached your ideal intake. If you are adapting your children's intake, don't forget that they will need less fibre than you to achieve the same results.

Give the process time. It may take two or three weeks for your gut to get used to a changed rhythm. Then you will start to look, and feel, better. Don't give in to the temptation of adding the amount of fibre which you feel you may need, all at once. If you do, you will run the risk of feeling distinctly uncomfortable because of distension and 'wind' caused by the unaccustomed bulk in your gut. It is unpleasant and there is no need for it. If you increase your intake very gradually, as we have suggested, most of it can be avoided. Even if you experience a little discomfort for a day or two, it will soon pass! It is also important to drink plenty of water or similar clear fluids when you eat extra fibre. This will enable the fibre to stimulate your gut really effectively. You will then be able to gain the maximum benefits from your new-found 'natural' eating.

PART II · RECIPES

PROCESSES AND PRODUCTS

Long or repetitive recipes can be boring, and we want to give as varied and interesting a collection as possible—so we have decided not to reiterate some of the usual detail about the processes and products we all use most often.

The most important processes, we think, are preparing vegetables and fruit for eating and cooking so that they keep as much of their vital vitamin value as possible. Preparing vegetables and fruit properly is even more important than usual in a book like this where vegetables occur in unexpected places such as desserts. However, we are quite sure that you neither need nor want to be told dozens of times to skin an onion before cooking it. So we shall describe the basic preparation processes just once (page 64) and 'take them as read' in the recipes.

As for other processes, we have taken for granted that, if you are reading this book, you are interested in sensible cookery and are, almost certainly, a sensible cook. We shall assume, therefore, that you already know how to make a roux, French dressing and pastry; the difference between folding in and beating or blending; and how far to reduce a sauce to make a glaze. Sometimes, then, we shall simply tell you to use a basic cooking process, or to use your own favourite recipe for making a needed ingredient or garnish.

We propose to do much the same thing concerning basic products such as flour, salt and sugar. Instead of repeating precisely what to use in every recipe, we give below a list of 'standards' so that, unless a particular type of product is mentioned in the list of ingredients you can and should always use the same recommended 'basics' for all our recipes and keep them in stock in your store-cupboard. We hope that this will save you both time and money, and will encourage you to use what we believe to be sensible products in all your cooking.

STANDARD PRODUCTS TO USE

Flour
Plain wholemeal or wholewheat flour should be used unless another is suggested. Do not be misled by wheatmeal products which may well be made with flour of a higher extraction rate. White flour, self-raising flour or 'strong' flour are specified if needed.

Always sieve flour when making baked goods. There will be a marginally smaller quantity and a more aerated product than if the flour is just turned into a bowl. When you sieve wholemeal flour you will, of course, find particles of bran left behind in the sieve. Turn them back into the main mass. Doing this does not mean that your sieving has been futile; far from it. The whole mass of flour will have been lightened and will give you a lighter pastry, dessert or cake.

Yeast
Fresh yeast should be used if possible. We think it is easier and quicker to use than dried yeast, and one can tell more readily if it is still in peak condition. However, if hard to find, use half the quantity of dried yeast.

Baking powder
Commercial baking powder contains starch as well as bicarbonate of soda and cream of tartar but this need not prevent its use if more convenient than using your own mix. Use your own bicarbonate of soda/cream of tartar mixture if you wish.

Bread and breadcrumbs
Wholemeal bread and breadcrumbs should always be used unless otherwise stated.

Corn meal, maize meal and polenta
These are all the same thing. In our recipes we use the name which seems best suited to each dish. Use whichever product you can obtain most easily, regardless of what it is called. Yellow corn meal (maize meal, polenta) gives a more attractive-looking result in most dishes, but white meal can be used equally well if it is more convenient.

Rice
Brown rice should always be used. Take care that you really get brown rice, and are not fobbed off with unpolished rice masquerading as brown rice. Even though it is better than snowy polished rice, you will have been cheated.

Pasta
Wholemeal pasta—macaroni, spaghetti, etc.—should be used in all recipes.

Pastry
Wholemeal shortcrust pastry should be used unless otherwise stated. Unlike many books, the quantity of pastry suggested in our recipes always refers to prepared, ready-to-use pastry.

Fats
Slightly salted butter, hard block margarine or white vegetable fat can be used as you prefer unless otherwise stated.

Oils
We do not specify which type of oil you should use. Any pure vegetable oil can be used for salad dressings and for cooking other than frying; some people prefer the flavour of one to that of another. Frying is a different matter. Oils such as olive and walnut oil have a strong flavour and should only be used for frying if a piece of potato or bread is fried in the fat first to 'mop up' the smell. Olive oil, in particular, should only be used for frying at low temperatures because it has a very low 'flash point': it catches fire more easily than any other oil. It has been used in Southern Europe for centuries because it has always been the cheapest oil there; but we have alternatives which are cheaper, more stable and more safe, so keep olive oil just for salad dressings if you can. For frying, then, choose any safe oil with a high 'flash point'. Make sure that it is clean and has been kept well stoppered in a dark place, so that it is in good condition and will heat to the right temperature in the right time to give you crisp, fully cooked food.

Cheese
Use the best-quality cheese you can get. You will use less of a properly matured English Farmhouse Cheddar for instance than of a mild creamery-made one, so it will not really be much more costly, and its flavour has more vitality. If possible, buy Parmesan cheese in a block and grate it yourself when required; it will be much less harsh than the ready-grated product.

Cottage cheese and yoghurt
Natural, unflavoured cheese and natural low-fat yoghurt should be used unless the recipe specifies the use of 'cottage cheese with chives', or sweetened yoghurt, goat's milk or some other yoghurt.

Sugar
The recipes state which type to use. When we say 'sugar', however, we mean sugar and not a liquid form of sweetening such as molasses. Where brown sugar is advised, do try to use one of the natural muscovados or demerara sugar.

Honey
Clear honey should always be used unless stiff honey or honeycomb are specified.

Fruit and vegetables
The weights we give for fresh vegetables are always for unprocessed vegetables, just as you buy or pluck them, unless otherwise stated. For instance, if the weight of peas is for the peas after shelling they will be described as 'shelled peas' in the list of ingredients. For detail on the preparation of fruit and vegetables see page 64.

Fruit juices
Unstrained lemon, orange, pineapple and other fruit juices should be used unless strained juice is specified.

Lemon and orange rind
Use the thin yellow outer rind, and pare it off with a potato peeler, unless the recipe directs you to use peel. Then use the whole peel, including both rind and pith.

Dried fruit and raisins
Although seeded raisins are juicier and better flavoured than the smaller seedless ones, they can be too heavy for light-textured mixtures. The recipes do therefore sometimes specify seedless raisins. Remember that they are much improved if soaked in hot water for 10–15 minutes before they are used.

Parsley, other herbs and spices
Fresh parsley should always be used. Use fresh herbs too, unless otherwise stated, whenever you can; and if you have to use a dried herb, halve the quantity suggested in the recipe. (Of course, when a dried herb is specified, the right amount to use is given.) Freshly bought herbs and freshly ground spices should be used whenever possible. For instance, nutmeg grated off a whole nutmeg into a dish is far tastier than the ready-ground product you can buy. If you keep a varied collection of herbs and spices, as we hope you do, try to use them quickly. Dried herbs and spices soon lose their flavour and aroma; after two or

three months, they taste and smell like dust and are absolutely useless.

Salt
Sea or kitchen rock salt is best for all cooking except for baking and in soufflés; use table salt in spite of its additives for these, and whenever it is suggested for some special reason.

Pepper
Freshly ground black pepper should be used unless otherwise directed.

Garam masala
Ideally one should create one's own from fresh spices, but few Europeans are able to obtain all the correct ingredients or have the skill or time to do it properly. One can buy ready-ground garam masala in Indian grocery stores, and—processed as it is—it is still a better product than curry paste or powder made for the European market.

Vinegar
Cider vinegar should be used unless otherwise stated.

WEIGHTS AND MEASURES

In this book, we give British Standard imperial measures followed by metric equivalents in brackets. Use whichever you know best, but take care not to mix them when you follow a recipe—use all imperial or all metric measures in making that particular recipe because the quantities do not match each other exactly.

Do not be concerned by the two measures; the differences are very slight. All it means is that in making large batches of baked goods or a large-sized cake the metric quantity or size will be slightly smaller.

Do not be concerned, either, when you find that metric quantities vary in relation to their imperial equivalents. We have sometimes varied them deliberately. Where we felt that it would be wise to have slightly more rather than less of a particular product, say carrots, we may have suggested using 500 g as the metric quantity in relation to 1 lb, instead of the more usual 450 g. Again, the differences are usually slight and are not important. After all, however scrupulously you weigh your carrots, the quantity of scarred flesh and rough skin you have to scrape off afterwards will vary a little every time. Similarly, scales can vary in the quantities they record, for instance if they are not quite clean. In fact it is not possible—and luckily is not necessary—to measure accurately to the last drachm or scruple when cooking ordinary meals in a domestic kitchen.

This does not mean that you should leave things wildly to chance. Do, please, use scales and measuring spoons; metric ones are now quite easy to obtain. Being *reasonably* accurate can make all the difference between success and failure, especially in making baked goods. Remember that all spoons should be level spoons unless otherwise stated. Fill the spoon slightly heaped, then slice off the heaped contents with a knife-blade to the level of the rim.

Since we have gathered our recipes from many different lands, with different measuring systems, we have sometimes had to use odd quantities, especially of liquids. We have rounded these to quarter, half and full pints whenever possible. Where it has been difficult to do, we have expressed the quantities as fluid ounces. You will find these marked on almost all measuring jugs. Fluid ounces are easy to measure; only remember that they do not bear any weight relation to ounces of solid goods. They are measures of volume, not of weight.

Most cookery books use two standard sets of nearly matching, rounded-off imperial and metric quantities as parallels. We have followed the British Standard practice of taking 25 grams (25 g) as the parallel to 1 ounce and 25 millilitres (25 ml) as the parallel to 1 fluid ounce. Here, in tabular form, are the sets of parallel measures we have used for weight, volume and length:

1 oz (ounce)	25 g (grams)	1½ lb	700 g
2 oz	50 g	2 lb	900 g or 1 kg
3 oz	75 g		(kilogram)
4 oz	100 g	2¼ lb	1 kg or 1·05 kg
5 oz	125 g	2½ lb	1.1 kg
6 oz	150 g	3 lb	1.3 kg
7 oz	175 g	3½ lb	1.5 kg
8 oz	200 g	4 lb	1.8 kg
12 oz	300 or 350 g	4½ lb	2.0 kg
16 oz or 1lb (pound)	450 or 500 g	5 lb	2.3 kg

1 fl oz	25 ml (millilitres)	1¾ pints	1 litre
2 fl oz	50 ml	2 pints	1.1 litres
3 fl oz	75 ml	2½ pints	1.4 litres
4 fl oz	100 ml	3 pints	1.7 litres
5 fl oz or ¼ pint	125 ml	3½ pints	2 litres
10 fl oz or ½ pint	250 or 300 ml	4 pints	2.3 litres
15 fl oz or ¾ pint	375 ml	4½ pints	2.5 litres
20 fl oz or 1 pint	500 ml	5 pints	2.8 litres
1½ pints	850 ml		

⅛ inch	3 mm (millimetres)	6 inches	15 cm
		6½ inches	16 cm
¼ inch	5 mm or 0.5 cm (centimetres)	7 inches	17 cm
		7½ inches	18 or 19 cm
½ inch	1 cm	8 inches	20 cm
1 inch	2.5 cm	9 inches	22 or 23 cm
2 inches	5 cm	10 inches	25 cm
3 inches	7.5 cm	11 inches	27 cm
4 inches	10 cm	12 inches	30 cm
5 inches	12.5 cm		

We have also used as parallels:

¼ teaspoon	½ × 2.5 ml spoon	1 dessertspoon	1 × 10 ml spoon
½ teaspoon	1 × 2.5 ml spoon	1 tablespoon	1 × 15 ml spoon
1 teaspoon	1 × 5 ml spoon		

and we have given you the accepted parallel oven heats in degrees Fahrenheit (for British and American electric cookers), degrees Celsius (for Continental and metric-marked electric cookers) and in Regulo markings (for gas cookers).

Helpings

One last point. We have estimated the number of helpings each recipe will supply (or the size or weight of a cake or loaf). In the case of vegetables and salads, we have explained which are side-dish helpings and which are main-course ones. People's appetites, however, vary very widely indeed. The number of helpings we have suggested should, therefore, be taken only as a broad guide.

BREAKFASTS WITH FIBRE

OATMEAL PORRIDGE

For 4 helpings, use:

> 1¼–1½ pints (700–850 ml) water
> 5 oz (125 g) medium oatmeal
> salt

Bring the water to the boil in a heavy pan. It should be bubbling well to prevent the oatmeal clotting when stirred in. Sprinkle in the oatmeal slowly. Stir with a wooden spoon until it is all stirred in. Lower the heat, cover the pan, and simmer very gently for 10 minutes. Add a good sprinkling of salt, cover again, and simmer for another 10 minutes.

Serve in 4 cold porringers, with separate small bowls of cream, milk or buttermilk for each person. Honey and a knob of butter can be added to the porridge although not traditional.

THERMOS PORRIDGE

This is a good winter breakfast to leave ready for anyone who has to get up extra early.

For 3–4 helpings, use:

> 8 tablespoons (8 × 15 ml spoons) coarse oatmeal
> 1–2 tablespoons (1–2 × 15 ml spoons) natural wheat bran
> ¾ pint (375 ml) water
> 1 tablespoon (1 × 15 ml spoon) seedless raisins
> ¼ teaspoon (½ × 2.5 ml spoon) salt
> ½ teaspoon (1 × 2.5 ml spoon) muscovado sugar

Put all the ingredients into a saucepan and mix them well. Heat slowly to boiling point, and boil gently, uncovered, for 5 minutes. While boiling, rinse out a large, wide-necked Thermos flask or insulated food container with boiling water.

Tip the porridge into the flask, stopper it securely and leave it for 8–10 hours or overnight. Turn it out into bowls and serve it with milk, cream or buttermilk, and with extra sweetening if you wish.

POLENTA (CORN-MEAL PORRIDGE) (Basic recipe for cooked corn meal)

Polenta, corn meal and maize meal are different names for the same grain product. Mealie meal is another name for it. Whatever name it goes by, cook it in the same way.

For 4 helpings, use:

> 4 oz (100 g) polenta (corn meal, maize meal)
> 1 teaspoon (1 × 5 ml spoon) salt
> 1¼ pints (700 ml) water

Mix the polenta and salt to a smooth paste with a little cold water. Bring the 1¼ pints (700 ml) water to the boil in a saucepan, and add the polenta paste to it. Stir with a wooden spoon until the mixture thickens.

Have ready a double boiler containing simmering water. Put the thickened porridge in the top of the boiler, over the water. Cover the pot and cook very gently for at least 40 minutes, or longer if you want a thicker polenta.

Sweeten and serve with hot milk as a porridge; or use polenta with a savoury sauce, or as a side dish with meat, fish or vegetables instead of pasta or rice.

Note: Although this way of cooking keeps it moister than cooking it over direct heat, any polenta is drier than oatmeal porridge, so a spoonful of butter is often stirred into it before serving.

MUESLI

Modern muesli was developed and made popular in Switzerland by Dr Bircher-Benner in the early part of this century, but it is much older than that. Dry or soaked grain mixed with fruit, herbs or nuts has been a staple dish of all peasant peoples in Europe throughout their written history. Some archaeologists claim that ancient Neolithic man almost certainly lived mainly on a mixture of crushed grain, raw fruit and nuts which he could gather easily as he wandered. They say that his brain developed and he survived because of the almost complete nourishment it provided.

Properly-made modern muesli is a similar, almost complete food. The ingredients tempt one to call muesli 'summer porridge' because, like hot porridge, it basically consists of crushed grain (conventionally, oats) eaten with milk or cream, sugar, honey or treacle. But it is a more complete, more nourishing food than hot porridge: it is uncooked, so has lost no nutrients through being heated; and, more important, a high proportion of its bulk should consist of fresh, raw summer fruit and/or dried fruit and nuts. By using wheat or other flaked grains instead of oatflakes, muesli can be varied in even more ways than hot winter porridge; it can be rich or bland, tangy or nutty.

To make Dr Bircher-Benner's muesli, soak any unprocessed grain for 12 hours, but chop or grate and combine it with the grain only just before you eat it. Use honey as sweetening if you can: dark molasses or Barbados sugar make the paler ingredients look murky. Use milk, fresh cream or whole-milk natural yoghurt, rather than condensed milk or commercially cultured low-fat yoghurt. You can thicken ordinary milk if you wish by stirring in a little dried skimmed milk powder, or sieved curd cheese creamed with a little of the whole milk. (Curd cheese gives you tangy milk.)

We confess that we are not always as scrupulous as this in making our own muesli. We use bought, natural low-fat yoghurt for instance, if we have some to use up. Try, however, as we do, to add a few fresh sweet herbs, such as chopped mint, and use them to vary your muesli sometimes. Even a sprig set in the centre of the dish changes its appearance and give it a scent which promises good flavours to come. The list below gives suggestions for some of the alternatives you can use.

GRAIN	FRUIT	LIQUID (add honey)
oatmeal	dried apples	top of the milk
oatflakes	pears	single or whipping cream
flaked wheat	plums	milk mixed with sieved curd cheese
cracked wheat (burghul)	apricots	evaporated milk
barley flakes	well-drained fresh orange segments	natural yoghurt mixed with single or double cream
millet flakes	well-drained, chopped fresh pineapple	cultured buttermilk, alone or mixed with single cream or top of the milk
soya flakes	chopped fresh apricots or plums dipped in lemon juice	
add a teaspoon (1 × 5 ml spoon) wheat germ to any of them if you wish	pipped grapes	
	whole fresh blackberries	
	whole or halved fresh strawberries	

EASY MUESLI

This muesli uses foods which are easy to obtain, although not quite as nutritious as some of the alternatives we have recommended.

For 4 helpings, use:

> 1 large or 2 small sharp dessert apples
> fresh lemon juice
> 1 oz (25 g) seeded raisins or dried apricots
> 1 oz (25 g) sultanas
> 4 oz (100 g) quick-cooking rolled oats (dry for crunchiness)
> 1 tablespoon (1 × 15 ml spoon) natural wheat bran
> 1 oz (25 g) demerara sugar
> 3 tablespoons (3 × 15 ml spoons) chopped mixed nuts
> about ¼ pint (125 ml) natural yoghurt, bought or home-made

Core, then dice or grate the apple without peeling (we prefer dicing it). Toss the dice or shreds in the lemon juice at once. Chop the dried fruits. Mix together the oats, bran, dried fruit and sugar. Drain the apple well, and mix it in. Chill for about 10 minutes, not more. Turn the mixture into 4 porringers and sprinkle with the nuts. Let each person add his own yoghurt to moisten the dry ingredients.

RICH MUESLI

For 4 helpings, use:

> 4 oz (100 g) natural wheat flakes
> water
> 1 large or 2 small sharp dessert apples
> orange juice
> 1 oz (25 g) seeded raisins
> 4 stoned fresh dates, about 2 oz (50 g), if you wish
> 6 tablespoons (6 × 15 ml spoons) double cream
> 2 tablespoons (2 × 15 ml spoons) natural yoghurt, bought or
> home-made
> 2 tablespoons (2 × 15 ml spoons) clear honey or fruit syrup
> from stewing fruit
> 3 tablespoons (3 × 15 ml spoons) finely chopped almonds,
> hazelnuts or walnuts

Soak the wheat flakes for 15–30 minutes in fresh cold water, and drain them well. Squeeze them dry. Just before the muesli is required, prepare the fruit (including the fresh dates) as in the recipe for Easy Muesli above. Mix together the cream, yoghurt, and honey or syrup. Complete as for Easy Muesli.

YOGHURT

Natural yoghurt can be used in so many different ways with cereals, vegetables and fruit that it is worth keeping in stock. If you want cheap, well-flavoured or thick yoghurt, without the trouble of shopping for it every day or so, you should make your own.

For a large group, it may be worth your while to buy special yoghurt 'starter'. For one family, an easier, if slightly more expensive way is to 'start' your yoghurt with commercial natural yoghurt, and then use your own yoghurt to 'start' new batches of yoghurt. When, after 2–3 months, the yoghurt bacillae weaken and die (when your 'starter' fails to make reasonably thick, pleasant yoghurt within 6 hours) begin afresh with a new carton of commercial yoghurt.

If you make your own, you can vary the texture of your yoghurt by using a treated milk, for example:

1. Raw, pasteurized or homogenized fresh milk, boiled and cooled to 115°F (46°C) (for average yoghurt).
2. Boiled or sterilized milk with 2 oz (50 g) dried skimmed milk powder in each 1 pint (500 ml) milk (for thicker yoghurt).
3. Boiled and cooked water with 3 oz (75 g) dried skimmed milk powder in each 1 pint or just less (400–500 ml) water (for thick yoghurt).

There are several ways to incubate the yoghurt (to make the yoghurt bacillae grow in the milk and turn it into yoghurt). The most usual way is to wrap the yoghurt container in a warmed blanket, and put it in an airing cupboard with an even temperature or near a radiator; or you can use an electric yoghurt-making machine. A third way is to incubate the yoghurt in a wide-necked Thermos flask. Whichever you use, the surrounding temperature needs to be slightly warmer than the yoghurt itself.

AVERAGE YOGHURT (Blanket method)

    1 pint (500 ml) treated milk (type 1)
    1 tablespoon (1 × 15 ml spoon) low-fat natural yoghurt, bought or home-made

Boil the milk and cool to 115°F (46°C). Put a small quantity in a bowl rinsed in boiling water. Whisk in the yoghurt, then stir in the remaining milk thoroughly. Cover the bowl tightly, wrap it in a warmed blanket, and keep it at a temperature of 110°F (43°C) for about 4 hours. Check whether a curd has formed. If not, incubate the yoghurt for up to 6 hours. If it has not curded then, it will not succeed.

    When the curd has formed, let the container cool at room temperature, then store it in the refrigerator. Use within 36 hours.

THICK YOGHURT (Thermos method)

    3 oz and 1 tablespoon (75 g and 1 × 15 ml spoon) dried skimmed milk powder
    1 pint (500 ml) water
    1 tablespoon (1 × 15 ml spoon) low-fat natural yoghurt, bought or home-made

Put the skimmed milk powder in a 1½-pint (850 ml) bowl. Bring the water to the boil, and boil it for about 2 minutes. Mix enough water with the milk powder to make a smooth cream. Then add, gradually, the rest of the water, beating out any lumps. Cool the mixture to 115°F (46°C).

    While cooling, rinse out a wide-necked Thermos flask or insulated food container with boiling water. Do *not* use a narrow-necked flask—the yoghurt curd will break up when you try to get it out.

    When the milk has cooled to the correct temperature, stir in the yoghurt. Pour the mixture into the flask and stopper it securely. Leave it for up to 8 hours, or overnight for a thicker yoghurt.

    Cool, store and use like Average Yoghurt, above.

If you wish, you can flavour and add fibre to your yoghurt after making it, by stirring or putting into it very finely chopped chives, blanched spring onion, coarsely ground nuts or chopped fruit such as pineapple. Do not disturb the yoghurt more than you can help, and leave it to firm up afterwards; it will liquefy when stirred. Use yoghurt with additions as soon as possible, because it will 'go off' quickly.

STEWED FRUIT

The best way to stew both fresh and dried fruit is to make a syrup first, then steep the fruit in it for a while, and finally poach the fruit gently in the same syrup for as short a time as possible. Serve hot or cold in the syrup.

Soft berry fruits such as raspberries or cultivated blackberries do not need stewing. If you want to serve them in liquid, just pour a warm or hot syrup over them, and serve them as they are when it has cooled. For 1 lb (450 g) fruit, make the syrup by boiling about 4 oz (100 g), sugar, any type you like, and a strip of lemon rind in ¼ pint (125 ml) water for 6 minutes; skim it, cool it to finger-hot, and pour it over the fruit. Take out the lemon rind.

If you want to cook other fresh fruits, make a similar syrup but less sweet. Vary the flavour if you wish; in each ½ pint (250 ml) water, use any of the following to replace the lemon rind: a 1-inch (2.5 cm) piece of cinnamon stick; 4–5 whole allspice berries; a blade of mace; a little coarsely grated nutmeg or ground mixed spice. Make a syrup with about 4 oz (100 g) sugar and ½ pint (250 ml) water for 1 lb (450 g) of most fruits, or ¾ pint (375 ml) water for very hard fruits. Remember that any brown sugar will give the fruit some of its own colour and flavour.

Dissolve the sugar in the water by stirring it over gentle heat. Bring it to the boil, then leave it off the heat for 6–7 minutes. If you have time, put a lid on the pan and let it stand until quite cold, then steep the cut-up fruit in the syrup for an hour before you stew it. It will keep its shape and colour better.

If you need to cook the fruit straight away, cut it up as soon as you take the syrup off the heat. Take out any cores or stones and put the fruit into the syrup at once. When the syrup has stood for the full 6–7 minutes, put it back on the heat with the fruit, and simmer the fruit very gently indeed (with a lid on the pan) until it is tender.

The time required will vary a great deal with the fruit. Tender ripe apple pieces may take only 4 minutes, hard cooking pears may take 2–3 hours. As soon as the fruit is cooked, lift it out of the syrup with a slotted spoon, and put it in a heatproof bowl. Either strain the syrup over the fruit or boil it down to thicken slightly, before straining and pouring over the fruit.

If you want to stew dried fruit such as apple rings, apricots or figs, soak the fruit for 24 hours in cold water, with one of the flavourings above, until it is tender. Strain off the cooking juice and taste it to see how much sweetening it needs. Prunes and figs will probably need none at all, apples or apricots may need about 1 oz (25 g) sugar or honey in each 1 pint (500 ml) juice. Heat the juice to dissolve the sweetening, then simmer it for 7–10 minutes to make a syrup, and pour it over the fruit while still hot.

WHOLEMEAL BRIOCHE OR RASTON ROLLS

For 1 large brioche or 12 rolls, use:

> 14 oz (400 g) wholemeal flour (strong flour if possible)
> 1 teaspoon (1 × 5 ml spoon) salt
> 2 teaspoons (2 × 5 ml spoons) light soft brown sugar
> 2 oz (50 g) butter or margarine
> 1 oz (25 g) fresh yeast or 1 tablespoon (1 × 15 ml spoon) dried yeast
> 4 tablespoons (4 × 15 ml spoons) warm water
> 3 eggs
> beaten egg to glaze

Shake the flour, salt and 1 teaspoon (1 × 5 ml spoon) sugar together in a bowl. Rub in the fat. Blend the fresh yeast with the warm water or sprinkle the dried yeast on to the water. Stir in the second teaspoon (1 × 5 ml spoon) sugar. Beat the eggs into the yeast liquid and stir into the flour to form a soft dough. Turn on to a lightly floured surface and pummel well for about 5 minutes or until the dough is smooth and elastic, no longer sticky. Put the dough in a large, lightly oiled polythene bag and leave in a warm place to rise for about 1 hour or until doubled in bulk. Grease a 7–8-inch (17–18 cm) round cake or brioche tin or twelve 2¾–3¼-inch (12 × 7–8 cm) small deep bun tins. Knead the dough again until firm. For a large brioche, shape the dough into a ball and put it in the cake or brioche tin. If making small rolls, cut the dough into 12 equal-sized pieces, and cut a bit the size of a cherry from each. Form each larger piece into a ball and put it in a small tin. Make a shallow hole in the centre with your thumb and place the 'cherry' there as a knob. Put the tin or tins on a baking sheet and cover with the polythene bag. Leave in a warm place for about 30 minutes or until the dough is light and puffy. Brush with beaten egg and bake in a very hot oven, 450°F (230°C) Gas 8, for

12–15 minutes for the rolls, 35–40 minutes for the one large brioche.

SOYA HALF-HOUR BREAD

For one 1½-lb (700 g) loaf, use:

8 oz (200 g) wholemeal self-raising flour
6 oz (150 g) white self-raising flour
2 oz (50 g) soya flour
1 teaspoon (1 × 5 ml spoon) salt
1 teaspoon (1 × 5 ml spoon) baking powder
2 oz (50 g) soft tub margarine
½ pint (250 ml) milk or water
margarine for greasing

Shake the three flours thoroughly in a mixing bowl with the salt and baking powder. Rub in the fat, or beat it in with an electric hand mixer. Then mix or beat in enough liquid slowly to make a soft dough. Knead the dough for 2 minutes; dust your hands with extra wholemeal flour if it is sticky. Grease a loaf tin about 8 × 4 × 3 inches (20 × 10 × 7.5 cm) in size. Turn in the dough, and press it well down into the corners; you do not want creases in your loaf. Level the top smoothly. Make three diagonal slashes on the top of the loaf, to make it rise quickly and evenly. Bake it at 425°F (220°C) Gas 7 for 30 minutes or until it has risen, is golden brown and sounds hollow when tapped. Cool on a wire rack, and wrap closely when cold. Eat within 3–4 days—its nutty flavour 'dulls' after that.

The dough also makes 12–14 good small Soya Rolls, to eat warm, split and buttered. Shape them on a surface dusted with wholemeal flour and bake them on a lightly greased baking sheet for 15–18 minutes. Have them for breakfast with crisp bacon or for supper with kippers, herrings or a spicy green vegetable dish.

LIGHT MEALS—
DOUBLE-DUTY RECIPES

Starters

CARROT COCKTAIL

For each helping, use:

> 1 medium carrot
> 2 medium spring onions, white parts only
> ½ teaspoon (1 × 2.5 ml spoon) grated orange rind
> celery salt
> pepper
> cayenne pepper
> 1 oz (25 g) cottage cheese

Top and tail the carrot, and shred or grate it coarsely. Finely chop the white parts of the spring onions (keep the green parts for another salad or a hot vegetable dish). Mix the carrot, onion and grated orange rind with a fork, then season well. Mix in the cottage cheese thoroughly, with the fork; it should just bind the vegetable mixture. Pile into individual stemmed glasses if serving as a dinner starter or on lettuce leaves on a small plate as a lunch dish. Chill briefly but serve without much delay, with Benné Biscuits (page 41) if a starter or with Clappers (page 116) spread with butter as a lunch dish.

CRUDITÉS ON A TRAY

Small pieces of raw or blanched vegetables are enough filling to be a main course, particularly if teamed with other small items such as hard-boiled egg segments or anchovy fillets. They satisfy the eye for a start, especially if laid in a flat, decorative pattern on a tray. A chequerboard pattern like the ground-plan of a herb garden is attractive.

Cut the vegetables into any bite-sized shapes which suit you; but avoid split, soaked, overchilled items such as radish 'roses' or 'lilies' which have lost their food and flavour value. Blanch any bits which may discolour, or which are hard rather than crisp. Dip apple, pear or peach cubes in lemon juice or French dressing; salt cucumber, black radish or aubergine and leave on a tilted plate for 30 minutes before use.

Choose from the suggestions below, making your selection varied but not too large. It is better to offer a small choice of items cut up with care and seasoned individually. Do not simply grind salt and pepper over everything. Taste each vegetable, and decide what it needs (perhaps a few drops of orange juice) to bring out its full character.

Buttered wholemeal rolls make a tray of crudités with a bowl of dressing or a spicy dip into a full supper course.

Choice

apple cubes, dipped in lemon juice

pear cubes, dipped in French dressing

young carrot, cut into matchsticks or longer spears

cauliflower spriglets, blanched

celery stalks, split lengthways then cut into 1½-inch (4 cm) sticks

cucumber cubes, salted and drained (thin slices go soggy)

sweet green or red pepper, cut in thin strips

spring onions with about 1 inch (2.5 cm) green stem

fennel bulb, thinly sliced and blanched

black olives, stoned

fresh dates, stoned

broccoli florets, cooked

celeriac or kohlrabi, coarsely grated, sprinkled with French dressing

tomatoes, cut into 8 segments

baby cherry tomatoes, split, hollowed and stuffed with soft cheese

pickled onions or walnuts

small cocktail gherkins

DIPS FOR CRUDITÉS

A dip is a very thick savoury sauce, usually based on sieved soft cheese or a vegetable purée, softened with cream, soured cream or mayonnaise, and well spiced. It should be thick and creamy enough to cling to whatever is dipped into it, and flavoured to suit the 'dunkers' you are using.

Here are proportions for a useful basic dip which can be adapted and flavoured in many different ways.

For 8–10 fl oz (200–250 ml) dip, use:

> 8 oz (200 g) home-made curd cheese or cottage cheese
> 4–6 fl oz (100–150 ml) natural yoghurt or soured cream
> 4 tablespoons (4 × 15 ml spoons) thick Tomato Cocktail Sauce (page 139)
> a few drops onion or garlic juice and/or Tabasco
> salt and pepper

Sieve the cheese, yoghurt or cream and tomato sauce together and season well. Chill for at least 1 hour to let the flavours blend before use.

If the cheese is dry, or if you want to add a solid flavouring ingredient such as chives, grated carrot or crumbled blue cheese, increase the quantity of yoghurt or soured cream to give the consistency you want.

SWISS PEARS

For 4 starter or light main-course helpings, use:

> 2 cooking pears
> juice of 1 lemon
> 2 oz (50 g) Swiss Gruyère cheese
> grated rind of ½ lemon
> 1 dessertspoon (1 × 10 ml spoon) softened butter
> extra butter for greasing
> a sprinkling of paprika

Halve the pears lengthways without peeling them. Remove any pips and hard core with a pointed teaspoon. Pare a sliver off the rounded sides to make the pears stand level, cut side up.

Simmer the pear halves in water with the lemon juice for a few minutes but only until just softened at the edges. Drain thoroughly. Crumble the cheese and mix in the grated lemon rind and softened butter. Pile the mixture on the cut sides of the pears. Grease a shallow flameproof plate and lay the pears on it, cut side up. Grill under gentle heat until the cheese bubbles and browns a little. Sprinkle with paprika. Serve at once with toasted Crown Rye Bread (page 114).

CURRIED FRUIT COUPES

A carefree store-cupboard standby is a useful asset in one's repertoire. This one is colourful and can be made in a few moments from goods which are easily kept in stock.

For 8 starter or 4 main-course helpings, use:

For the curried mayonnaise and topping
    grated rind of 1 lemon
    4 tablespoons (4 × 15 ml spoons) fresh lemon juice
    2 teaspoons (2 × 5 ml spoons) clear honey
    1 teaspoon (1 × 5 ml spoon) curry paste
    12 tablespoons (12 × 15 ml spoons) mayonnaise

For the salad
    10 oz (250 g) Swiss Gruyère cheese
    4 tablespoons (4 × 15 ml spoons) seedless raisins
    1 × 7¾ oz (1 × 227 g) can pineapple rings
    2 tablespoons (2 × 15 ml spoons) flaked or slivered almonds
    4 or 8 maraschino cherries
    extra grated lemon rind as available (see recipe)

Make the curried mayonnaise first. Put 2 teaspoons (2 × 5 ml spoons) lemon rind in a small bowl. (Keep any extra grated rind aside for sprinkling on the salad.) Mix the rind with the juice, honey and curry paste in the bowl. Blend thoroughly, then mix in the mayonnaise. Cover the bowl and chill it until you need it.

Cut the Swiss Gruyère cheese into thin strips, ½ inch (1 cm) wide and 2½ inches (6 cm) long. Put them aside. Pour boiling water on the raisins, and let them stand for 5 minutes. Drain the pineapple rings and cut them into segments.

For main-course salads, put 4 tablespoons (4 × 15 ml spoons) of the curried mayonnaise in the bottoms of 4 stemmed saucer-glasses or dessert bowls (8 fl oz/200 ml size). Drain the raisins. Mix them with the pineapple segments and almonds. Arrange the cheese strips on end in the glasses or bowls, with the salad ingredients between them. Top each salad with a cherry, and sprinkle it with any extra lemon rind. For a dinner-party starter, divide the mayonnaise and salad between 8 small shallow glasses.

Serve with Benné Biscuits (page 41).

CORN-MEAL RAREBITS

For 8 slices or 24 fingers, use:

6–7 oz (150–175 g) Edam cheese
4 oz (100 g) salted peanuts
8 slices wholemeal bread
1 tablespoon (1 × 15 ml spoon) cooking oil
3 tablespoons (3 × 15 ml spoons) corn meal (polenta, maize meal)
½ teaspoon (1 × 2.5 ml spoon) salt
1 teaspoon (1 × 5 ml spoon) dry mustard
a good pinch of cayenne pepper
6 fl oz (150 ml) milk
2 teaspoons (2 × 5 ml spoons) Worcester sauce
2 tablespoons (2 × 15 ml spoons) chopped watercress leaves

Grate the cheese and chop the peanuts finely. Cut the crusts off the bread, and toast the slices lightly on both sides. Keep warm.

Heat the oil in a deep frying pan or skillet over low heat. Stir in the corn meal, salt, mustard and cayenne pepper. Then add the milk and Worcester sauce very slowly, stirring all the time to prevent lumps forming. Continue stirring over low heat until the mixture thickens; do not let it boil. Mix in the cheese and nuts, stir round briskly, and take off the heat at once. Spoon over the dry toast slices, cut into fingers if you wish, and serve sprinkled with watercress.

If you prefer, spoon the mixture into a container with a lid, cover it and let it mellow for at least 3 hours, or more, before using it.

BROCCOLI ROLL-UPS

For 4 helpings, use:

4 spears fresh broccoli or 1 × 9 oz pkt (1 × 225 g pkt) frozen broccoli
4 oz (100 g) cottage cheese with chives
4 thin slices lean cooked ham
1 egg
salt and pepper
4 tablespoons (4 × 15 ml spoons) wholemeal or high-bran breadcrumbs
4 teaspoons (4 × 5 ml spoons) margarine

Thaw the broccoli if frozen, and cook until just tender in a very little water. Cut off the stems. Spread 1 oz (25 g) cottage cheese over each ham slice. Place a cooked broccoli flower on each slice, and roll the ham round it. Beat the egg until liquid with the salt and pepper, and use to coat the ham rolls. Scatter the breadcrumbs on a sheet of paper, and roll the coated ham in them. Press the crumbs on firmly. Place the roll-ups on the grill rack, and dot each with 1 teaspoon (1 × 5 ml spoon) margarine. Grill, turning often, until the crumbs are crisp and browned on all sides. For supper, serve with any remaining broccoli, Baked Maize (page 88) and home-made mustard (page 138).

HERB TERRINE

For about 2½ lb (1.1 kg) terrine, use:

 1¼ lb (600 g) fresh spinach
 1 lb (450 g) streaky bacon rashers without rind
 1 medium onion
 1 clove garlic
 1 sprig each parsley and fresh rosemary (or ¼ teaspoon
  (½ × 2.5 ml spoon) dried rosemary)
 2 sprigs each (or ½ teaspoon (1 × 2.5 ml spoon) dried herb)
  marjoram, savory and basil
 1 large egg
 12 oz (300 g) sausage meat
 salt and pepper
 3 fresh or dried bay leaves

Cut off the stems of the spinach and cut out any coarse ribs. Cook the spinach gently in a little salted water for 6 minutes. Drain and squeeze it to get rid of as much water as possible. Chop it finely.

Finely chop 4 oz (100 g) of the bacon with the onion and garlic, and fresh herbs if you use them. (If using dried herbs, sprinkle them on the onion.) Mix all the chopped ingredients thoroughly. Beat the egg lightly and mix it in. Fork out any lumps in the sausage meat and mix in. Season well.

Line a 2¼-pint (1.2 litre) oven-to-table dish or pie dish with bacon, keeping aside enough rashers to cover the top of the dish. Press in the terrine mixture. Lay the three bay leaves on top, then cover lightly with the remaining bacon rashers. Stand the dish in a pan containing enough hot water to come half-way up its sides.

Bake at 350°F (180°C) Gas 4 for 1–1¼ hours. The terrine is done when it shrinks slightly from the sides of the dish.

About 15 minutes before the end of its cooking time, take off the top bacon rashers to let the terrine brown a little.

Eat the terrine hot, with dry toast, or put greaseproof paper and light weights on top and leave in iced water until cold.

Serve from the dish, cut in slices.

Soups

DRESSED ONION SOUP

For 4 helpings, use:

>   1½ lb (700 g) onions
>   1 pint (500 ml) milk
>   1 blade whole mace
>   a pinch of grated nutmeg
>   salt and white pepper
>   about ½ pint (250 ml) strong chicken or vegetable stock (page 135)
>   6 fl oz (150 ml) single cream
>   3 oz (75 g) cooked butter or haricot beans, puréed
>   a pinch of cayenne pepper
>   3 oz (75 g) dried dark brown rye breadcrumbs
>   2 oz (50 g) cooked spinach leaves or 16 cooked small asparagus tips (sprue)

Slice the onions. Simmer them in the milk with the mace, nutmeg and seasoning for 10 minutes, until they are just softened. Strain the liquid through a sieve into a measuring jug. Add enough stock to the milk to make 1½ pints (850 ml) liquid. Put back in the pan, and replace the onions. Cover the pan, and simmer gently for 30 minutes. While cooking, blend the cream with the bean purée.

Strain the soup into a clean pan. Sieve in the onions and any soft stock ingredients (or process in an electric blender and add to the soup). Stir in the creamy bean purée, and season with extra salt and a few grains of cayenne pepper. Reheat without boiling; when very hot, pour into heated individual soup bowls. Sprinkle rye crumbs all round the edge of each bowl, and put a small cluster of spinach leaves or asparagus tips in the centre. A decorative soup!

CABBAGE AND YOGHURT BROTH

This well-flavoured broth is almost as thick as a vegetable stew. Add to its protein value by substituting cooked soya beans for the macaroni if you wish.

For 4–6 helpings, use:

1¼ lb (600 g) firm white cabbage
1 onion, about 4 oz (100 g)
1 carrot, about 3 oz (75 g)
1 tomato, about 3 oz (75 g)
1 oz (25 g) bacon or chicken fat, or margarine
1½ pints (850 ml) vegetable stock (page 135)
2 oz (50 g) elbow cut wholemeal macaroni
salt and pepper
¼ teaspoon (½ × 2.5 ml spoon) paprika
¼ teaspoon (½ × 2.5 ml spoon) caraway seeds
¼ teaspoon (½ × 2.5 ml spoon) ground coriander
¼ pint (125 ml) natural yoghurt
1 tablespoon (1 × 15 ml spoon) beaten egg

Shred the cabbage, discarding the stalk and coarse ribs. Finely chop the onion, carrot and tomato, or process briefly in an electric blender. Melt the fat in a large stewpan. Add the onion, carrot and tomato, stir round, then cover the pan and simmer for 5 minutes. Add the cabbage. Mix the vegetables well, then pour in the stock. Bring to the boil, and stir in the macaroni and dry seasonings. Half cover the pan, and simmer for 15 minutes or until the cabbage and macaroni are tender.

Stir the yoghurt and beaten egg together until blended. When the broth is ready, taste it and season again if required. Remove broth from heat, and stir in the yoghurt and egg mixture.

Serve it while still very hot, with wholemeal rolls.

SUMMER TURNIP SOUP

For 4 helpings, use:

> 3 oz (75 g) wholemeal bread
> 3 medium white turnips, about 10 oz (250 g)
> 1 carrot, about 2 oz (50 g)
> 2 pints (1.1 litres) water
> salt and white pepper
> a small pinch of ground allspice
> 4 oz (100 g) fresh young spinach leaves
> a few young beet leaves or Brussels sprout tops if available
> 1–3 oz (25–75 g) butter (see recipe)

Remove crusts from the bread, then cut into ½-inch (1 cm) dice and set aside. Shred both root vegetables on the coarse holes of a grater. Add them to the water in a saucepan, with plenty of salt and pepper and a little allspice. Bring to simmering point, half cover the pan, and simmer until tender. Meanwhile, cut any tough ribs out of the leaves, shred them coarsely, and add them to the soup 6–7 minutes before the root vegetables are ready.

You can also add the bread dice if you like, and stir them in to make a thicker, porridgy soup like the old-style pottages on which this is based. However, they provide a more interesting texture and flavour contrast if you fry them in 2 oz (50 g) of the butter until golden all over, then scatter them on the completed soup.

Either way, taste for seasoning, then stir the remaining 1 oz (25 g) butter into the soup in small flakes just before serving. This way, the flakes should just melt. Scatter the golden fried bread dice, as suggested above, on each helping.

LENTIL SOUP WITH GINGER DUMPLINGS

For 6–8 helpings, use:

> ¾ lb (350 g) red lentils
> 1 large onion
> 2 tablespoons (2 × 15 ml spoons) vegetable oil
> 3½ pints (2 litres) vegetable stock (page 135)
> 1 stick celery
> 1 medium carrot
> 1 spiced herb bundle (page 136) including 2 cloves garlic
> salt and pepper

For the dumplings (makes 18)
4 oz (100 g) wholemeal self-raising flour
3 teaspoons (3 × 5 ml spoons) grated fresh ginger root
a good pinch of ground cumin
a sprinkling of salt
a grinding of pepper
2 oz (50 g) shredded suet or white vegetable fat
water to mix

Rinse the lentils. Chop the onion. Heat the oil in a large saucepan, add the chopped onion, and stir it with a wooden spoon until soft and lightly browned. Add the lentils, and stir for another 2 minutes to coat them. Have the stock heating on the stove, and when it is really hot pour it over the lentils. Bring it very slowly to the boil, then lower the heat to simmering point. Slice the celery and cut the carrot into matchsticks; add them to the simmering soup with the spiced herb bundle and a good sprinkling of seasoning. Continue simmering for about 45 minutes, until the lentils are soft.

Meanwhile, make the dumplings. Mix the flour and all four flavourings together thoroughly. Mix in the fat, then work in enough cold water to make a firm but pliant dough. Knead it well to smooth out any creases, then divide it into 18 equal-sized pieces. Form them into small balls. Drop them into the simmering soup 10–12 minutes before the end of the cooking time. Taste soup for seasoning before serving.

MUNG BEAN SOUP

Although most people only use them for sprouting, mung beans are not far short of soya beans in protein content, and are therefore a useful quickly prepared substitute for soya beans if you are in a hurry or have no cooked soya beans in stock. Their protein content makes this, for instance, a valuable main-course soup without meat or fish.

For 4 helpings, use:

5 oz (125 g) mung beans
1½ pints (850 ml) water
salt
1 onion, about 4 oz (100 g)
1 carrot, about 2 oz (50 g)

½ turnip, about 2 oz (50 g)
4 oz (100 g) French or runner beans, fresh or frozen (see recipe)
vegetable stock (page 135) as needed (see recipe)
pepper if needed
single cream if you wish
1 tablespoon (1 × 15 ml spoon) chopped chives or parsley

Soak the mung beans in the water overnight. Then simmer them in the same water, with a sprinkling of salt, for about 20 minutes or until they are tender but not broken. Skim well while cooking.

While cooking them, prepare the other vegetables. Chop or shred the onion, carrot and turnip. Slice fresh green beans.

Drain the cooked mung beans, and measure the cooking liquid. Make it up to 1¾ pints (1 litre) with vegetable stock. Put the liquid back in the pan with the mung beans, root vegetables and fresh green beans if you are using them. Bring to simmering point, half cover the pan, and simmer for 20 minutes or until the vegetables are tender. If you are using frozen beans add them, unthawed, for the last 10–12 minutes only.

Taste, and add extra salt and a grinding of pepper if you wish. Serve with a swirl of cream and/or a sprinkling of bright green chopped chives or parsley on each helping.

And To Go With Them:

DEVILLED BISCUITS OR TOASTS

'Devils' were used in eighteenth-century England to revive the thirst of gentlemen during long claret-drinking evenings. Devilling mixtures were used in Victorian days to make last night's leftovers (such as pheasants' legs) presentable for breakfast. Now, spread very thinly on biscuits or toast, these mixtures make good party snacks or crisp offerings to serve with creamy soups.

For 8–10 biscuits or toasts, use:

2 dessertspoons (2 × 10 ml spoons) anchovy essence
a pinch of cayenne pepper
¼ teaspoon (½ × 2.5 ml spoon) curry powder
¼ teaspoon (½ × 2.5 ml spoon) grated nutmeg
1 teaspoon (1 × 5 ml spoon) mixed English mustard
1 teaspoon (1 × 5 ml spoon) clear honey

8–10 any thin dry unsweetened biscuits or 5 slices wholemeal
bread from a tin loaf
butter for spreading

This is a fairly hot Victorian devilling mixture. Use black pepper
instead of cayenne or use slightly less anchovy essence if it is too
strong for your taste.

Mix together the anchovy essence, spices, mustard and honey.
Taste, and adjust the flavour if you wish. Warm the biscuits in a
cool oven; or cut the crusts off the bread slices, cut them in half
and toast them lightly on both sides. Spread biscuits or toast
pieces with butter, then very thinly with devilling mixture.
Reheat, if you wish, under a low grill or in the oven for a few
moments only. Serve in a folded napkin while still hot.

Note: This mixture keeps well in an airtight pot or jar for at least
3 weeks, so you can make a large quantity for a party ahead of
time.

BENNÉ BISCUITS

For 20–22 biscuits, use:

4 oz (100 g) wholemeal shortcrust pastry (page 124)
cayenne pepper or ground cumin for sprinkling
table salt
½ tablespoon (3 × 2.5 ml spoons) sesame seeds
1 egg yolk, beaten
extra sesame seeds for topping

Roll out the pastry into a rectangle ⅛ inch (3 mm) thick. Sprinkle
with cold water, then with cayenne pepper or cumin and salt.
Sprinkle the ½ tablespoon (3 × 2.5 ml spoons) sesame seeds over
half the surface. Fold over the other half of the pastry to cover the
seeds. Re-roll the pastry about ¼ inch (0.5 cm) thick and cut out
into 2-inch (5 cm) rounds. Brush the rounds lightly with egg
yolk, then sprinkle with a few extra seeds. Put them on a lightly
greased baking sheet, and bake at 375°F (190°C) Gas 5 for 10–12
minutes. Cool on the sheet. Store in an airtight tin; re-crisp in a
low oven just before serving if you wish. Serve as snacks with
drinks, or offer with soup (especially with clear or cream soups).

Savoury Dishes for Brunch, Lunch, High Tea or Supper

WHOLEMEAL CHEESE SOUFFLÉ

For 4 helpings, use:

> 2½ oz (60 g) margarine
> ¾ oz (20 g) wholemeal flour
> ¼ pint (125 ml) milk
> 3 eggs
> 3 oz (75 g) finely grated Gruyère or mild Cheddar cheese
> salt
> a pinch of cayenne pepper
> mixed English mustard to taste
> 1 tablespoon (1 × 15 ml spoon) extra finely grated Gruyère or Cheddar cheese

Prepare a 6-inch (15 cm) soufflé dish by tying round it a folded band of paper, 5 inches (12.5 cm) high, to support the soufflé as it rises.

Use ½ oz (15 g) of the margarine to grease the inside of the band. Melt the rest of the margarine gently in a fair-sized saucepan. Stir in the flour and cook together gently for 3 minutes without letting the flour brown. Stir in the milk gradually, stirring briskly to prevent lumps forming, and continue stirring until the mixture thickens smoothly. Remove from the heat and cool slightly.

Separate the eggs. Beat the yolks lightly, and stir them quickly into the sauce, blending thoroughly. Beat in the cheese and seasonings. Heat the oven to 400°F (200°C) Gas 6.

Beat the whites with a pinch of table salt until they hold stiff peaks. Stir 1–2 tablespoons (1–2 × 15 ml spoons) into the sauce to slacken it, then fold in the rest lightly but thoroughly. Turn gently into the prepared dish, sprinkle with the extra cheese and bake for about 25 minutes.

SPINACH QUENELLES

These little spinach puffballs are both delicately flavoured and decorative. They make a beautiful dinner-party starter or a lovely light meal served heaped in warmed soup bowls. Here, we bill them as a main course; serve them on a bed of wholemeal pasta rings with a plain green salad.

For 4 helpings, use:

1 lb (450 g) fresh spinach
4 oz (100 g) butter
6 oz (150 g) low-fat curd cheese (*not* cottage cheese)
2 eggs
2 tablespoons (2 × 15 ml spoons) double cream
2 oz (50 g) 81% extraction flour
1 oz (25 g) finely grated Parmesan cheese
¼ teaspoon (½ × 2.5 ml spoon) ground coriander
salt and pepper

Put the spinach in a saucepan with a little salted water, and heat gently with a tight lid on the pan until the leaves are just tender. Drain, and squeeze out all the water you can with your hands. You should have about 6 oz (150 g) well-pressed spinach. Chop it finely. Melt 2 oz (50 g) of the butter in a saucepan, stir in the spinach, toss well and cook for 3 minutes, still stirring. Take the saucepan off the heat, and rub the curd cheese through a sieve into the pan. Stir in well. Now beat the eggs until liquid and mix them with the cream. Mix together the flour, grated cheese and coriander. Stir the egg mixture and flour mixture alternately into the spinach, blending them in thoroughly but lightly. Season well. Spread on a flat plate, cover, and chill for 2 hours.

Shape the spinach mixture into small balls. Lower them gently, a few at a time, into a saucepan containing salted water which is only just moving. Poach them for about 10 minutes. They will puff and swell, rising to the surface. Scoop them out gently with a slotted spoon, drain them, and put them on a bed of hot, cooked, wholemeal pasta rings, if serving them as a main course. Keep hot under buttered paper. While poaching the last few quenelles, melt the remaining butter. Pour it over the quenelles and serve them while still glistening.

MUSHROOM RAGOÛT

For 3–4 helpings, use:

4 eggs
12 oz (300 g) large flat mushrooms
4 oz (100 g) button mushrooms
salt
4 fl oz (100 ml) claret or other red wine
4 oz (100 g) butter

2 dessertspoons (2 × 10 ml spoons) flour
¼ teaspoon (½ × 2.5 ml spoon) grated nutmeg
¼ teaspoon (½ × 2.5 ml spoon) ground mace
chopped parsley

Hard-boil the eggs. While boiling them, chop all the mushroom stems. Put the large mushrooms and the chopped stems in a saucepan, sprinkle with salt, and pour 4 tablespoons (4 × 15 ml spoons) of the wine over them. Cover the pan, and simmer for a few minutes until the mushrooms are just tender.

Cut 3 oz (75 g) of the butter into small pieces. Remove the whole mushrooms with a slotted spoon. Add the rest of the wine and the butter pieces to the pan. Let the butter melt. Season the flour with the nutmeg and mace, and stir it in. Simmer, stirring, until the sauce thickens. Replace the whole mushrooms, cover the pan and keep it warm over very low heat.

Put a small piece of the remaining butter in each button mushroom cap and grill gently until just tender. While grilling, shell the hot eggs, holding them in a cloth. Cut them neatly in halves and pile them in the centre of a warmed flat serving dish. Spoon the mushroom ragoût from the pan round them. Edge the ragoût with grilled mushrooms, and put one or two among the eggs. Sprinkle the eggs with bright green, chopped parsley. Serve at once, very hot, edged with small triangles of wholemeal toast.

HOT SWEET-SOUR SALAD

Stir-fried dishes are often cooked at the table. Prepare the ingredients a short time ahead, and arrange them on one or two plates to look like flat posies of flowers. For the cooking, use a heavy-bottomed deep frying pan, wok or skillet, set on an adjustable burner. These dishes are cooked and served just like a fondue except that you need both high and low heat.

For 4 main-course helpings, use:

2 medium carrots
2 thin slices fresh ginger root
1 clove garlic
1 sweet green pepper
1 medium onion
2 sticks young celery
3 oz (75 g) bean sprouts

3 tablespoons (3 × 15 ml spoons) white wine vinegar
2 oz (50 g) light muscovado sugar
1 tablespoon (1 × 15 ml spoon) medium-dry sherry
2 tablespoons (2 × 15 ml spoons) vegetable stock (page 135)
2 tablespoons (2 × 15 ml spoons) vegetable oil
salt and pepper

Cut the carrots in slivers about 1½ inches (3.5 cm) long. Blanch in salted water for 1–2 minutes, then drain. Finely chop the ginger root and garlic together. Seed the pepper, and cut in 1-inch (2.5 cm) squares. Halve the onion lengthways, and cut in strips about ½ inch (1 cm) wide. Slice the celery. Put the bean sprouts in a bowl, pour boiling water over them, shake, then drain them. Pat dry with soft kitchen paper.

Arrange the carrot, ginger and garlic on one plate, the rest of the vegetables on another. Put them on the table where you will cook.

Heat the vinegar and sugar in a small metal jug standing in a pan of simmering water. When the sugar is melting, remove the jug, and stir in the sherry and stock. Cover the jug, and put it on the table.

When ready to eat, heat the oil in a large, deep frying pan. Put in the carrot, ginger and garlic. Fry, stirring round, for about 2 minutes. Add the pepper, onion, celery and bean sprouts, and stir them in the hot oil for 2 minutes, turning them over. Add the vinegar mixture and stir for another 2 minutes. Season. Turn into a warmed dish. Serve with newly made Soya Half-Hour Bread (page 29) as a supper dish.

Note: This salad is also a stimulating dish to serve at a barbecue party with grilled meats and chunks of wholemeal bread.

BAKED CHAKCHOUKA

There are many versions of this well-known Middle Eastern egg dish. The one we have chosen saves you any last-minute frying. In some others, whole eggs are cooked with the vegetables and oil on top of the stove. Make the chakchouka in a shallow metal or ceramic dish with lug handles, which is presentable at table.

For 6 helpings, use:

1 sweet green pepper
1 medium onion

2 large courgettes, about 6 oz (150 g) each
salt
2 medium tomatoes
1 clove garlic
4 tablespoons (4 × 15 ml spoons) vegetable oil
6 eggs
a good pinch of ground coriander or cumin
a good pinch of cayenne pepper
chopped parsley

Seed the pepper. Slice both the pepper and onion into thin strips. Quarter the courgettes lengthways, then cut in ½-inch (1 cm) slices. Sprinkle them with salt, and put in a nylon sieve to drain. Slice the tomatoes and grate the garlic over them.

Heat the oil in a flameproof, oven-to-table dish about 8 inches (20 cm) deep. Add the onion and pepper, and simmer with a lid or plate on the pan until the pepper strips soften. Stir in the courgettes and tomatoes, cover and continue simmering until they soften. Meanwhile, beat the eggs until liquid, and season them with salt, spice and cayenne. Heat the oven to 425°F (220°C) Gas 7.

Take the pan of vegetables off the heat. Uncover and cool it for 2 minutes, then quickly stir in the eggs. Mix well. Bake in the oven, uncovered, for 10 minutes or until the egg mixture is lightly set. Sprinkle with parsley, and serve at once from the dish.

SABBATH SPROUTS

Originally this was a side dish using only vegetables, designed to go with Sunday night's cold roast beef or with shepherd's pie. You can use it as a vegetarian dish, if you prefer, by leaving out the bacon rashers and frying the beans and sprouts in margarine alone. If you do this, use extra margarine to grease the baking dish.

For 4 helpings, use:

1 lb (450 g) prepared young fresh Brussels sprouts or frozen
      sprouts
1 or 2 onions, about 6 oz (150 g)
4 back bacon rashers without rinds, if you wish
2 oz (50 g) margarine or more if needed
4 tablespoons (4 × 15 ml spoons) cooked soya beans

salt and pepper
a good pinch of grated nutmeg
2–3 tablespoons (2–3 × 15 ml spoons) toasted oatmeal or
   crispbread crumbs

Use enough fresh sprouts to give you 1 lb (450 g) after trimming.
Simmer the sprouts in very little unsalted water until just tender.
Drain. Slice the onion into thin rings.

Fry the bacon, if using it, in a frying pan large enough to hold
the sprouts. Remove the fried bacon, leaving the fat in the pan,
and chop coarsely. Use the fat in the pan to grease a shallow
oven-to-table dish which will hold the sprouts and other ingredients comfortably. Melt 1 oz (25 g) of the margarine in the frying
pan. Add the sprouts and beans and fry them gently, turning
them over, until the sprouts begin to brown. Lift out with a
slotted spoon, and put in the greased dish in an even layer.
Season well with salt, pepper and nutmeg. Add the bacon if
using it.

Melt the remaining 1 oz (25 g) margarine in the frying pan, and
fry the onion rings in it until lightly browned. Drain, and place on
the sprouts. Scatter the oatmeal or crispbread crumbs over the
dish, and sprinkle with any fat left in the pan. Reheat for 10–15
minutes at about 350°F (180°C) Gas 4. Serve hot.

APPLE-STUFFED PEPPERS

Adults may want a whole tangy pepper each, but they can easily
be cut in half for a child's or a light helping. A sustaining main
course with rice, the peppers make an equally good, lighter dish
by themselves.

For 4 helpings, use:

   4 large well-formed sweet green peppers
   1 small sweet red pepper
   1 small cooking apple
   2–3 dessertspoons (2–3 × 10 ml spoons) dry white wine or
      still cider
   4 large cup mushrooms
   3 oz (75 g) Swiss Gruyère cheese
   1 oz (25 g) butter
   1 oz (25 g) flour
   8 fl oz (200 ml) milk

2 tablespoons (2 × 15 ml spoons) soft wholemeal breadcrumbs
salt and pepper
a pinch of grated nutmeg
extra butter for greasing

Cut the tops off all 5 peppers. Discard the stems and seeds but
keep the caps. Trim the bottoms of the green peppers so that they
stand upright. Blanch all the peppers and caps in boiling water
for 3 minutes only, then drain.

Core and chop the apple, and mix it with the wine or cider.
Leave to soak. Remove the mushroom stems and put caps aside.
Chop the stems with the blanched red pepper and its cap. Grate
the cheese.

Melt the 1 oz (25 g) butter, and stir in the flour. Stir them
together over gentle heat for 2 minutes. Then gradually stir in the
milk, and continue stirring until it boils. Cook gently, still stirring, until the sauce is very thick, and drags from the sides of the
pan. Remove from the heat and cool for 5 minutes. Add the apple
with the wine or cider, the chopped-pepper mixture, breadcrumbs and cheese. Mix together and season well.

Grease a baking tin with extra butter. Fill the peppers with
most of the stuffing, replace their caps and stand them upright in
the tin. Fill the mushroom caps with the rest of the stuffing, and
add them to the tin. If you have stuffing left over, refrigerate it for
use as a pancake filling or rarebit mixture. Bake the peppers and
mushrooms for 25 minutes at 300°F (150°C) Gas 2.

When ready, cluster the peppers together in the centre of a
serving dish with the mushrooms round them. Serve at once,
with buttered wholemeal toast or, as a more solid main dish, with
brown rice.

SCOTCH FAGGOTS

For 4 helpings, use:

4 chicken livers or 4 oz (100 g) lamb's liver in one thick slice
½ tablespoon (3 × 2.5 ml spoons) frying oil
8 oz (200 g) sausage meat
½ tablespoon (3 × 2.5 ml spoons) French mustard
salt and pepper
fine oatmeal for coating
1 egg
oil for deep frying

Remove any sinew or membrane from the livers or piece of liver. Cut lamb's liver into 4 neat chunks. Heat the ½ tablespoon (3 × 2.5 ml spoons) frying oil in a frying pan, and turn the livers or chunks in it until they are browned on all sides and almost cooked through. They should still be quite pink in the centres. Cool them.

Mix the sausage meat with the French mustard, salt and pepper, and pound it until quite smooth. Divide it into 4 portions. Roll each liver or piece of liver in fine oatmeal, then wrap it in sausage meat, enclosing it completely. Roll the sausage-meat balls in a little more fine oatmeal. Beat the egg until liquid, and coat the sausage-meat balls with it. Then roll each ball in oatmeal again, pressing it on firmly. Chill the balls for at least 30 minutes. Heat the oil for deep frying, and fry the balls at 365°F (185°C) Gas 5 until they are crisp and golden brown. Drain them on soft kitchen paper. Eat hot or cold.

These faggots make an excellent tray meal when hot. Cold, they are a satisfying change from sandwiches for a packed meal.

CORN-MEAL PANCAKES

These pancakes are light and fluffy. They make a delicate, almost spongy 'stack' (see page 50).

For 4–5 helpings (14–16 pancakes), use:

> 3 tablespoons (3 × 15 ml spoons) corn meal (polenta, maize meal)
> ¼ teaspoon (½ × 2.5 ml spoon) salt
> 3 tablespoons (3 × 15 ml spoons) cold water
> 7½ fl oz (190 ml) boiling water
> ½ tablespoon (3 × 2.5 ml spoons) butter
> 5 oz (125 g) plain white flour
> ¼ teaspoon (½ × 2.5 ml spoon) baking powder
> a good pinch of bicarbonate of soda
> 2 eggs
> ½ pint (250 ml) milk
> ½ tablespoon (3 × 2.5 ml spoons) cider vinegar
> 2 tablespoons (2 × 15 ml spoons) vegetable oil
> your choice of stuffing

Mix the corn meal, salt and cold water in a saucepan, and stir in the boiling water. Cover and simmer for 3–4 minutes, until thick.

Turn into a bowl, stir in the butter and leave to cool. Keep covered. Mix the white flour with the baking powder and bicarbonate of soda.

Separate the eggs. Mix together the milk and vinegar. Stir the milk and vinegar into the corn meal, then beat in the egg yolks and oil. Add the flour mixture slowly, and beat until smooth, or process briefly in an electric blender. Whisk the egg whites until semi-stiff and fold them in.

Heat barely enough oil in a shallow 8-inch (20 cm) frying pan to coat the bottom. Spoon in and spread enough batter to cover the pan thinly. Unlike ordinary pancakes, cook slowly and thoroughly, as the pancakes are fragile. Cook until the underside is golden brown, then turn over with a palette knife to cook the second side. Stack the pancakes on a plate and keep warm if serving hot, or lay flat on soft kitchen paper to cool. Fill with any non-melting soft stuffing or cheese.

STACKED SAVOURY PANCAKES

For 6–8 helpings, use:

7 Corn-Meal Pancakes (page 49)

For filling 1
8 tablespoons (8 × 15 ml spoons) cottage or low-fat curd
   cheese mixed with ½ sweet green pepper, finely chopped
salt and pepper

For filling 2
3 large firm tomatoes, thinly sliced, sprinkled with chopped
   fresh or dried basil
salt and pepper

For filling 3
3 hard-boiled eggs, chopped, bound with 5–6 teaspoons
   (5–6 × 5 ml spoons) soured cream or thick yoghurt
salt and pepper

For the topping
3 fl oz (75 ml) Vegetable Cream Sauce (page 139)
toasted flaked peanuts

Make the pancakes, and mix the three fillings in separate bowls. Lay one pancake flat on a serving plate. Spread with half Filling 1. Cover with a second pancake and put half the tomato slices on it

(Filling 2). Top with a third pancake, spread with half filling 3. Repeat the layers ending with the last pancake. Cover with foil, and reheat in the oven at 325°F (160°C) Gas 3 for about 15 minutes. Heat the vegetable cream sauce, pour it over the pancake stack, and sprinkle with the peanuts. Serve hot, cut in wedges like a cake.

Note: For our method of toasting nuts, see page 128.

FULL-VALUE MAIN DISHES

HERRINGS WITH APPLE SLICES

For 4 helpings, use:

> 4 herrings or small mackerel
> salt and pepper
> 2 lemons
> 1 sharp dessert apple, e.g. Granny Smith
> 1 oz (25 g) fine oatmeal
> 2 tablespoons (2 × 15 ml spoons) cooking oil

Split the fish right down the belly, and clean if not already gutted through the gill. Rinse the insides briefly and pat dry. Season the fish inside with salt and pepper. Grate the rind of both lemons and squeeze the juice of one. Put the juice in a saucer. Core the apple, but do not peel. Cut four thin slices right through the apple, making four rounds. Cut each in half, making semi-circles. Dip them at once in the lemon juice, coating both sides, then sprinkle them with half the lemon rind. Fit two semi-circles of apple side by side inside each fish.

Make diagonal slits, three on each side, in the skin of the fish. Mix together the remaining lemon rind and the oatmeal and coat the fish with the mixture. Lay the fish on a grilling rack. Sprinkle with a little lemon juice and with most of the oil. Grill for 6–8 minutes until the upper side is cooked and browned. Turn the fish over, sprinkle with the remaining oil, and cook for 4–5 minutes until quite tender.

Serve with triangles of *dry* brown toast (because the fish is fatty) or with brown rice (page 81).

SESAME-GLAZED FISH FILLETS

For 4 helpings, use:

>4 thick pieces of white fish fillet (cod, haddock or coley),
>   5–6 oz (125–150 g) each
>flour for dusting
>pepper
>frying oil as needed
>2 oz (50 g) fine-cut orange marmalade (not jelly marmalade)
>1 oz (25 g) sesame seeds
>4 teaspoons (4 × 5 ml spoons) natural wheat bran
>4 thin slices fresh orange

Skin the pieces of fish and pat them dry. Dust them well with flour. Grind a good sprinkling of black pepper over both sides of each fillet. Sprinkle with oil. Place on the grill rack, skinned side up, and grill gently for 4–5 minutes until almost cooked through. While grilling, mix the marmalade, seeds and bran thoroughly with a fork. Turn the fillets over when ready. Spoon the marmalade mixture over them. Replace under gentle grilling heat, and grill for about 4 minutes to cook the fish right through and to set the glaze. Watch carefully to make sure the seeds do not blacken. Place an orange slice on each fillet. Serve with sliced green beans flavoured with sage, or a celery and watercress salad.

BEEF STEW WITH DUMPLINGS

For 4 helpings, use:

>1¼ lb (600 g) stewing steak
>2 medium onions
>2 carrots
>1 oz (25 g) clean dripping
>3 tablespoons (3 × 15 ml spoons) flour
>1½ pints (850 ml) meat or strong vegetable stock (page 135)
>1 spiced herb bundle (page 136)
>½ teaspoon (1 × 2.5 ml spoon) dried mixed herbs
>salt and pepper
>
>*For the dumplings* (basic wholemeal dumpling recipe)
>4 oz (100 g) wholemeal self-raising flour
>a pinch of salt
>2 tablespoons (2 × 15 ml spoons) natural wheat bran

2 oz (50 g) shredded suet
1 teaspoon (1 × 5 ml spoon) chopped parsley
a good pinch of dried basil or sage
water to mix

Cube the steak. Chop the onions and slice the carrots. Heat the dripping in a saucepan or flameproof casserole. Add the meat and vegetables and turn them in the hot fat until they are well browned. Sprinkle in the flour, stir it in and simmer for 1 minute. Stir in the stock gradually. Add the spiced herb bundle. Bring to simmering point. Add the herbs and seasoning, then cover and simmer for 1–1¼ hours.

While simmering, mix the dry ingredients and fat for the dumplings, bind to a firm dough with water, and shape into 8 small balls. Roll them in extra flour, drop them gently into the stew and simmer for another 15–20 minutes. Serve the stew at once.

TOMATO DUMPLINGS

For 4 helpings, use:

4 large firm tomatoes
salt and pepper
12 oz (300 g) wholemeal shortcrust pastry (page 124)
2 teaspoons (2 × 5 ml spoons) dried thyme or basil
egg for glazing
fat for greasing
flour for dusting

For the meat filling
6 oz (150 g) minced beef
1 tablespoon (1 × 15 ml spoon) capers
1 teaspoon (1 × 5 ml spoon) soy sauce
1 tablespoon (1 × 15 ml spoon) soft breadcrumbs
4 teaspoons (4 × 5 ml spoons) grated onion
4 teaspoons (4 × 5 ml spoons) finely chopped parsley
salt and pepper
¼ teaspoon (½ × 2.5 ml spoon) grated garlic if you wish

Cut the tops off the tomatoes and set aside. Scoop out all the seeds, juice and centre core flesh. Season the cavities lightly, then turn the tomato shells upside-down to drain.

Make the filling. Mix all the ingredients together thoroughly, and moisten with a little of the juice from the tomatoes.

Fill the drained tomato shells with the meat mixture, and replace the caps. Roll out the pastry about ¼ inch (5 mm) thick, and cut out 4 large rounds which will each enclose a tomato completely. You may have to make the fourth out of re-rolled trimmings. Sprinkle the rounds with the dried herb. Place a tomato, cap side up, in the centre of each round. Draw the pastry up round it to enclose it, pinching it into a tiny topknot at the top. Brush the pastry lightly with egg. Place the dumplings on a greased and floured baking sheet, and bake at 400°F (200°C) Gas 6 for about 20 minutes, until the pastry is well cooked through. Serve the dumplings at once with green vegetables.

GREEK RUSTIC LAMB

Originally, the meat was probably goat. It would have been heavily seasoned with fresh wild mountain herbs, and wrapped in paper smeared with olive oil. It was then cooked in a sealed earthenware pot.

For 4 helpings, use:

> 4 lamb steaks from leg or shoulder
> sea salt
> pepper
> chopped fresh marjoram, thyme or sage
> 2 large cloves of garlic cut in thin slivers
> lemon juice
> 2 tablespoons (2 × 15 ml spoons) natural wheat bran
> olive oil for greasing
> 4 oz (100 g) Feta cheese and cottage cheese with chives, mixed (see note)
> 2 large firm tomatoes
> ½ sweet green pepper

Buy lamb steaks about 5 × 3½ inches (12.5 × 8 cm) in size, and ½ inch (1 cm) thick. Snip the edges of the meat slices all round to prevent curling. Wipe and season well with salt, pepper and your chosen herb. Make slits in the meat and insert the garlic slivers. Sprinkle the meat with lemon juice and bran. Grease 4 sheets of foil, each large enough to enclose a meat slice completely. Lay one meat slice in the centre of each sheet. Crumble the cheese over the meat. Slice the tomatoes thickly and cut the pepper into 4 rings. Lay them on the cheese. Season well.

Enclose the lamb slices in the foil completely, like small parcels, so that no liquid can seep out. Place the parcels in an oiled baking tin. Bake for 2 hours at 300°F (150°C) Gas 2. Serve the foil parcels (which will contain plenty of cooking juices) straight on to the diners' plates without opening them. Plainly boiled macaroni is traditionally served with this dish.

Note: Imported Feta is so salty that it is best mixed with cottage cheese.

LAMB AND CHINESE LEAVES

A springtime dish for anyone who wants to cut down on fats and starches to get into trim for summer.

For 4–6 helpings, use:

> 1 × 3 inch (1 × 7.5 cm) piece cucumber
> 2 teaspoons (2 × 5 ml spoons) salt
> 4 oz (100 g) shelled garden peas
> 1 small leek, about 2 oz (50 g)
> ¼ head Chinese leaves, about 4 oz (100 g)
> 1 small onion, about 2 oz (50 g)
> 1 oz (25 g) butter or margarine
> 8 oz (200 g) minced lean stewing lamb
> 4 oz (100 g) cooked brown or red lentils
> ½ pint (250 ml) meat stock
> 2 tablespoons (2 × 15 ml spoons) tomato juice
> 1 teaspoon (1 × 15 ml spoon) ground garam masala
> pepper as needed

Cube the cucumber, put it on a tilted plate and sprinkle it with ½ teaspoon (1 × 2.5 ml spoon) of the salt. In a small pan, simmer the peas with another ½ teaspoon (1 × 2.5 ml spoon) of salt, until they are just tender. Thinly slice the leek, and shred the Chinese leaves. Slice the onion.

In a large deep frying pan or heavy saucepan, melt the fat, and fry the onion until it is soft and lightly browned. Add the meat, mashing it to break up any lumps, and turn it over in the fat until it is browned all over and well mixed with the onion. Drain and add the cucumber and peas, the leek, Chinese leaves and lentils. Pour in the stock, add the tomato juice, the remaining 1 teaspoon (1 × 5 ml spoon) salt, and the other flavourings. Half cover the pan, bring to simmering point, and cook gently for 15–20 minutes, or until the vegetables are cooked through but not mushy. Serve the lamb and its cooked 'salad' at once.

VEAL OR TURKEY OLIVES

For 4 helpings, use:

> 4 thin slices fillet or leg of veal (escalopes) or thawed, frozen Norfolk turkey fillets, about 4 oz (100 g) each
> 1 egg
> 4 teaspoons (4 × 5 ml spoons) natural wheat bran
> cooking oil for brushing fillets
> 1 teaspoon (1 × 5 ml spoon) finely chopped parsley
> grated carrot (see recipe)

> *For the stuffing*
> 3½–4 oz (80–100 g) grated carrot
> about 8 tablespoons (8 × 15 ml spoons) cottage cheese
> 2 teaspoons (2 × 5 ml spoons) natural wheat bran
> ½ teaspoon (1 × 2.5 ml spoon) grated orange rind
> a pinch of grated nutmeg
> salt and pepper

Nick the edges of the veal slices if you use them. Slice off the top layer of any turkey fillets too thick to roll up easily (use these for extra olives). Lay the veal or turkey slices on a board, and beat them flat and thin with a cutlet bat or rolling pin.

Work all the stuffing ingredients together, using just enough cheese to make a stiff mixture and seasoning generously. Spread on the fillets, and roll up each fillet like a small Swiss roll. Secure with cocktail picks if needed. Beat the egg, and brush the rolls with it; then coat the rolls lightly with the 4 teaspoons (4 × 5 ml spoons) bran.

Impale the rolls on long skewers and balance the ends of the skewers on the edges of a shallow baking tin, so that the olives hang over the tin. Sprinkle the olives very lightly with cooking oil and bake them at 350°F (180°C) Gas 4 for 30–35 minutes. While they are cooking, mix the chopped parsley with the extra grated carrot.

Serve the olives sprinkled with the carrot and parsley. They are good with mashed potatoes and garden peas as a main course, or with fruit chutney as a supper dish.

LIVER WITH ONION GRAVY

Cook a whole 3-lb (1.3 kg) liver even for a small family. It has a better flavour and will stay moister than small slices. It will not be wasted—cooled in its cooking liquid, it is even better cold than hot.

For 4 hot and 4–6 cold helpings, use:

> 1 whole calf's liver, about 3 lb (1.3 kg)
> 6 oz (150 g) back bacon rashers
> 1 medium onion
> 2 fresh bay leaves or 1 dried bay leaf
> ¾ pint (375 ml) chicken stock
> 3 fl oz (75 ml) white wine if you wish
> 2 tablespoons (2 × 15 ml spoons) butter
> 1 tablespoon (1 × 15 ml spoon) wholemeal flour
> ½ tablespoon (½ × 15 ml spoon) soy sauce or mushroom ketchup
> salt and pepper
> chopped parsley

Remove any tubes and membrane from the liver. Put it in a casserole. Cut the bacon rashers in half and cover the liver with them. Split the onion and lay it on top with the bay leaves. Heat the stock almost to boiling point and pour it into the casserole. Add the wine if you use it. Cover the casserole tightly. Cook in the oven at 350°F (180°C) Gas 4 for 45–55 minutes or until the liver is cooked but still moist and slightly pink inside.

Remove the casserole from the oven. Take out the onion, and chop or mash it into small bits. Put it in a small saucepan. Add 6 fl oz (150 ml) of the cooking liquid in the casserole. (Keep the liver warm in the remaining liquid.)

Blend the butter and flour to make a smooth paste. Heat the onion liquid almost to boiling point. Take off the heat, and stir in the butter–flour mixture in small spoonfuls, adding the soy sauce or ketchup. Stir until the butter melts; then return to gentle heat, and continue stirring until the sauce thickens. Taste, and season with salt and pepper.

Carve as many slices of liver as you need for the hot meal. (Leave the rest in the casserole with the remaining cooking liquid.) Place the hot liver in a warmed shallow dish, and pour the onion gravy over it. Cover with the bacon, and sprinkle with chopped parsley.

Note: Cover the casserole, and stand it in a pan of chilled water to cool quickly. When cold, store in the refrigerator. If left in its cooking liquid, the liver will taste almost like pâté de foie gras when sliced.

STIR-FRIED KIDNEY AND BEAN SPROUTS

This Far Eastern dish is prepared and cooked exactly like the Hot Sweet-Sour Salad on page 44.

For 4 helpings, use:

12 oz (300 g) bean sprouts
1 large thin slice fresh ginger root
1 medium onion, about 4 oz (100 g)
4 spring onions, both green and white parts
2 sticks celery
4 oz (100 g) calf's or lamb's kidney, skinned and cored
1 medium carrot
salt and pepper
2 tablespoons (2 × 15 ml spoons) chicken stock
2 tablespoons (2 × 15 ml spoons) medium-dry sherry
1½ tablespoons (2 × 10 ml spoons) cooking oil

Put the bean sprouts in a bowl, pour boiling water over them and shake well. Drain and pat dry with soft kitchen paper. Finely chop the ginger root. Halve the onion from top to root, then cut each half into lengthways strips about ½ inch (1 cm) wide. Thinly slice the spring onions, celery, and kidney. Coarsely shred the carrot.

Arrange the ginger root, onion and spring onion on one plate, the bean sprouts, celery, kidney and carrot on a second plate. Sprinkle them all lightly with salt and pepper. Mix together the chicken stock and sherry in a small jug, and put it, with the two plates, on the dining-table, together with the oil bottle and a cooking spoon.

When ready for the meal, heat the oil in a deep frying pan, wok or skillet set on an adjustable burner. Put in the ginger root, onion and spring onion, and stir for about 2 minutes until the onion strips begin to turn colour. Add the bean sprouts, celery, kidney and carrot, and continue stirring for 3 minutes, turning them over until they are all well coated and slightly fried. Pour in the stock and sherry, let them boil up, then simmer for 1–2 minutes. The liquid should be reduced almost to a glaze. Remove the pan from the heat, and serve the dish from it, at once, with hot, cooked brown rice (page 81).

NORTH AFRICAN FRUIT TAGINE

Another dish which has a tang of ginger and is eaten with rice. This one is very different, however, being long-simmered to blend its fruit and honey flavours. It is derived from one of Claudia Roden's recipes—or rather, from a mixture of two—in *A Book of Middle Eastern Food* (Thomas Nelson, 1968; Penguin, 1970).

For 6–8 helpings, use:

> 2 lb (900 g) boneless lean lamb or 4–6 fleshy chicken joints (see recipe)
> 1 medium onion
> salt and pepper
> ½ teaspoon (1 × 2.5 ml spoon) ground ginger
> 1 teaspoon (1 × 5 ml spoon) ground cinnamon
> 1 teaspoon (1 × 5 ml spoon) ground coriander or ½ teaspoon (1 × 2.5 ml spoon) allspice (with lamb)
> 1 tablespoon (1 × 15 ml spoon) dried mixed herbs (with chicken)
> 2 tablespoons (2 × 15 ml spoons) cooking oil or chicken fat
> 8 oz (200 g) prunes, well soaked, and stoned
> 1 lb (450 g) cooking or sour eating apples
> 2 tablespoons (2 × 15 ml spoons) clear honey
> 1 tablespoon (1 × 15 ml spoon) orange juice
> 1 tablespoon (1 × 15 ml spoon) grated orange rind

Make this succulent dish as spicy or as gentle as you like by adapting the quantities of the flavourings.

Cut the lamb into 1-inch (2.5 cm) pieces if you use it. If you use chicken, to serve 8 people, buy 4 large, 8–9 oz (200–225 g), joints and cut them in half. Chop the onion. Put the meat, onion, a little seasoning, the spices and any herbs you use in a large saucepan. Add the oil or fat, and just enough water to cover the ingredients. Bring slowly to the boil. Lower the heat to simmering point, and simmer gently until the meat is tender. Good-quality lamb will take about 2 hours, chicken about 1 hour. Add the prunes 45 minutes before the end of the cooking time. By the end, the cooking liquid should have become a rich sauce.

While cooking, core and slice the apples. When the meat is tender, add them to the dish with the honey and orange juice. Stir them in gently, and simmer for about 15 minutes until the sliced fruit is just tender. Do not let it get mushy. Taste and adapt the seasoning if you wish. Sprinkle each helping with a little orange rind, and serve with brown rice (page 81) or plainly cooked white beans.

GOOBER CHICKEN

For 4–6 helpings, use:

1 large roasting chicken, about 4 lb (1.8 kg)

For the Goober Stuffing
2 oz (50 g) soft wholemeal breadcrumbs
1 tablespoon (1 × 15 ml spoon) natural wheat bran
1 stick celery
2 oz (50 g) salted peanuts
1 onion
1 small carrot
3 oz (75 g) Cheddar cheese
salt and pepper
4 teaspoons (4 × 5 ml spoons) lemon juice
1 egg
2½ oz (65 g) butter

Make the stuffing first. Mix together the breadcrumbs and bran. Finely chop the celery, peanuts, onion and carrot. Grate the cheese. Mix all these stuffing ingredients together, adding the seasoning and 2 teaspoons (2 × 5 ml spoons) lemon juice. Beat the egg and melt the butter. Use the egg and about 1 tablespoon (1 × 15 ml spoon) of the butter to bind the stuffing mixture.

Stuff the chicken. Truss it and brush it with the rest of the butter, then sprinkle it with the remaining 2 teaspoons (2 × 5 ml spoons) lemon juice. Put it in a baking tin and bake it at 375°F (190°C) Gas 5 for 1½–2 hours, depending on its weight.

Serve the chicken with cauliflower or with runner beans in white sauce.

Note: Goober Stuffing is also good as a filling for a medium-sized marrow (2¼–2½/1–1.1 kg) or for pancakes.

LUCKY DIP CHICKEN

For 4 helpings, use:

> 4 chicken joints, about 6 oz (150 g) each
> 2 oz (50 g) natural wheat bran
> ½ teaspoon (1 × 2.5 ml spoon) crushed dried rosemary
> ½ teaspoon (1 × 2.5 ml spoon) grated orange rind
> salt and pepper
> 4 fl oz (100 ml) tomato juice
> 1 teaspoon (1 × 5 ml spoon) orange juice
> 1 teaspoon (1 × 5 ml spoon) lemon juice
> margarine or cooking oil as needed

> *For the sauce*
> 8 fl oz (200 ml) tomato juice
> 1 dessertspoon (1 × 10 ml spoon) orange juice
> 1 dessertspoon (1 × 10 ml spoon) lemon juice
> a few grains of salt if you wish

Skin the chicken joints and dry them well. Shake together in a
bowl the bran, rosemary and orange rind, and season with a little
salt and pepper. Mix 4 fl oz (100 ml) tomato juice and the teaspoons (5 ml spoons) of orange and lemon juice in a shallow bowl
or soup plate. Dip the chicken joints in the tomato mixture, then
in the bran mixture, and coat them well.

Grease or oil a baking tin which will hold the chicken comfortably, with space between each piece. Lay the chicken pieces in
the tin, fleshy side up. Dot all over with extra margarine or
sprinkle well with oil. Bake at 350°F (180°C) Gas 4 for 30–35
minutes without turning. Check that the chicken is cooked
through by running a thin skewer into one joint; it should come
out without a trace of pink.

While baking the chicken, simmer the juices for the sauce in a
small saucepan for 5 minutes. Taste and add a little salt if you
wish.

Serve the chicken joints with Savoury Polenta Cakes (page 88)
and with the hot sauce in a sauce boat.

VEGETABLE MEDLEY

Getting the Best out of Vegetables and Fruit

We are dealing with both vegetables and fruit in this section because so many of their features and processing methods are the same. The different kinds of vegetables and fruit we eat can provide, between them, most of the essential nutrients we get from other foods. But, more important, both give us vitamins and minerals which we cannot get easily in any other way.

However, both vegetables and fruit begin to lose their vitamin value as soon as they are harvested, and go on losing it steadily while they lie about; even faster if they are cut up, and then wait to be used. Since almost all these invaluable vitamins lie just under the coverings of most fruits and vegetables, peeling or rough scraping simply means throwing the best part of their food value into the garbage bin.

One more hazard: soaking in water leaches out the precious vitamins, and boiling them for any length of time does so still more. Some experts say that salt fosters the process, so that vegetables should only be salted after cooking. Perhaps the saddest waste of good food is a peeled, shredded vegetable, left to soak in a saucepan of salted water for some hours, then boiled until as soft as porridge.

Ideally, then, you should gather vegetables and fruit out of your own garden, process and cook them *minimally* at once, and serve them straight away.

This way of handling vegetables and fruit was probably easy in the Middle Ages, but it is seldom open to us now. Even a wise country housewife with a large garden does not go out and pull carrots in evening dress just as her guests arrive! City and flat dwellers have little chance of ground-to-table harvesting, although nowadays much ingenuity goes into the use of minimal space to grow *something*. However, everyone can take certain common-sense steps to see that they serve foods with as many nutrients as possible. If you have no garden, at least try to see that the vegetables you buy have come from the latest delivery to your supplier. We don't suggest that you rush out to the shops half an hour before every meal to get them, but do try to use non-imported green vegetables and soft or stone fruits on the day you buy them. Root vegetables, and fruits with tough skins such as citrus fruits, are more robust. Imported vegetables and fruits may well have been journeying or in storage for so long that a day or two longer will not make much difference to many of them.

PREPARING VEGETABLES

If you handle your fresh produce wisely, you will save yourself a lot of work and have more intriguing, better-flavoured vegetable dishes. No matter what vegetable you are dealing with, just rinse or scrub it and dry it briefly, then cut out any blemished parts and remove withered leaves; only some leafy vegetables, and leeks, may need breaking apart or cutting before you can rinse out the dirt. Leave others whole until you cook or eat them.

By all means, cut up the clean vegetables just before cooking them if you need or want small bits; you will actually save vitamins by the shorter cooking time. However, whether cooking them or eating them raw, don't shred or grate them more finely than you need to.

Then cooking! You can boil, steam, braise, grill or fry vegetables like any other food. But if you cook them in water (or in stock which we prefer) use as little as possible, and, as a rule, season your vegetables after cooking rather than before; the vitamin content (some people maintain) will be higher, and the flavour will be more vital. You may well be surprised at how little liquid and seasoning you need, especially when you 'short-cook' them. Cook most frozen vegetables in very little liquid without thawing them first. Even then, they will take less time to cook than fresh vegetables.

One of the joys of cooking vegetables is that, although there are so many of them and each has a unique flavour, colour and texture, one can use the same few, simple basic methods to cook almost all of them. They can even be cooked in the same pot, although, of course, tougher or woodier vegetables such as roots must be put in before delicate leafy ones. We do not practise this mixing in our own everyday cooking because we think the flavours and textures of the vegetables are more interesting when they are cooked separately and combined at the last moment. But if space on the stove is at a premium, it can be done.

Old and new vegetables, familiar friends and novelties! Here are our suggestions for preparing them. Obviously we haven't room to deal with every vegetable by name, but common sense will tell you which vegetables belong to each group below. Use these steps when you prepare vegetables for any recipe in this book.

Cleaning

All vegetables

1. *Pick over* vegetables, take out any twigs or yellowed leaves (e.g. watercress, parsley). Cut off root or root end of stalk (e.g. radishes, cauliflower). Take off leaf or stem if there is one. 'Top and tail' or cut off spiky or roughened ends (e.g. green gooseberries—excellent as a vegetable—French beans, celeriac).
2. *Rinse* off any loose outside soil or dirt under a cold running tap. Scrub roots and tubers only if very dirty (e.g. carrots, potatoes). Hold leaves of green vegetables open to let tap water run between them, or separate leaves from stalk if very dirty and rinse in a sieve. Make two cuts at right angles down through green tops of leeks so that green leaf parts open in fronds like a palm, for easier washing. Toss pulses (e.g. haricot beans) in a sieve under the tap to wash off dust.
   Pat vegetables dry with soft kitchen paper.
3. *Strip* off any papery outer sheath (e.g. spring onion, garlic); cut off any withered leaf-tops (e.g. spring onion, leek) or withered outer leaves; discard these. Take off coarse outer leaves if not wanted, but keep for stock;
   or
   Shell peas, pod broad beans, string runner beans—process similar vegetables likewise;
   or
   Scrape any blemishes out of root vegetables or fruit (e.g. apples) used as vegetables. Scrape off bits of coarse or rough skin. Do not peel unless the recipe directs it.
4. Rinse again, briefly, if dirty, before cutting up. Pat dry.

Cutting Down to Size

Green leafy vegetables e.g. cabbage, lettuce, Chinese leaves
Separate leaves from stalk if only flat, tender or heart leaves are needed. Keep stalk for crudités (page 30) unless woody.

Cut out and discard coarse ribs; they are usually woody. Break ribs of lettuce or Chinese leaves if you need flat salad leaves.

Cook or blanch whole leaves and shred after cooking whenever possible.

Shred by hand or in a food processor just before cooking or blanching for a casserole, salad or slaw. Do not use an electric blender—unless you want pulp. Shred coarsely unless the recipe directs otherwise.

Green 'flower' vegetables e.g. broccoli, cauliflower
Keep clusters as big as practical as a rule. For mixed vegetables and salads, divide into tiny spriglets with knife-tip or scissors. Do not pull apart—the heads may crumble.

Root and tuber vegetables e.g. carrots, potatoes, Jerusalem artichokes
Just occasionally, you may have to peel before cooking. Use a potato peeler, to peel as thinly as you can. Always shred coarsely.

Stalk and 'bulb' vegetables e.g. celery, fennel, onion, spring onion
Scrape old broad stems of celery to 'string' them. Slice bulbs rather than separating the fleshy leaves for cooking or blanching; single leaves go flabby. Slice all these vegetables thickly unless the recipe demands thin slices. Do not mince or process in an electric blender. Chop, if possible, in a deep bowl, using a sickle-shaped chopping knife. Always chop both the green and white part of spring onion unless the recipe directs otherwise. Keep green leaf fragments of fennel for adding to chopped parsley.

Seed and fruit vegetables e.g. marrow, pumpkin, tomato
Do not peel before cooking; if skin is still tough (e.g. on a big pumpkin) after cooking, do it then. Slice in thick chunks. If cutting into rings, scoop out seeds with a tablespoon.

Treat any large squash like marrow; cut off the narrow end of Crook-Neck Squash to make it fit your pan. Leave small squash such as Gem Squash whole, or cut in half, hollow out seeds and use as 'shells' for stuffing. Use the same recipes for any kind of squash; just adjust the cooking time to the size.

Remember that winter squash, which have hard rinds, keep well; summer squash should be used quickly.

As a rule, leave seeds in tomatoes. For a smooth purée, cut the fruit in quarters lengthways, then gouge out liquid and seeds with your thumb into a bowl (use for a sauce), leaving the flesh intact.

Legumes and pulses e.g. shelled peas, broad beans, haricot beans Leave whole. Rinse if necessary to remove dust, and check over for small stones and decayed peas, beans, etc.

QUICK-COOKING VEGETABLES

To save vitamins, any vegetable should be cooked for as short a time as possible. One can cook vegetables very quickly indeed by frying or grilling; but more often we need vegetables cooked without fat, or with only a little fat, to complement other dishes or to serve cold in salads. So we need to 'quick-cook' vegetables with liquid.

'Short-Cooking'

If one cooks vegetables whole or in big chunks, they should always be cooked with as little liquid as possible. Use vegetable stock (page 135), tomato juice or Tomato Cocktail Sauce (page 139) as the liquid instead of water; the vegetables will be beautifully seasoned, and any remaining stock will be aromatic and full-flavoured. (Any extra sprinkled seasoning, such as lemon rind or juice, should be added to the vegetables after cooking.) Vegetables such as spinach, marrow, pumpkin, sliced onions and mushrooms may need no liquid at all or only just enough to cover the bottom of the pan.

Brief-Dipping

A good way to 'quick-cook' vegetables is the one we have called brief-dipping. For this, the vegetables must be sliced, shredded or grated, which does involve vitamin loss—however, in compensation, they need only a very short cooking time. The idea behind brief-dipping is the same as that of Japanese *nabe* or at-the-table cookery. First, blanch any vegetables whole which are likely to be tough or bitter; few should need it. Slice the vegetables thinly and evenly (this is important) or shred or grate them, and break up florets. Season the vegetables with lemon juice, wine or soy sauce if you think they need tenderizing or flavouring. If, as is usual, you cook a mixture of vegetables, arrange them on platters, in the order in which they will go into the pot. Remember that roots must go in first. If cooking at the table, which is fun, arrange the ingredients in decorative patterns.

When you are ready to eat, put a little well-flavoured stock in a heavy saucepan or a deep pot (such as a fondue Bourguignonne pot) over a quickly adjustable heat source—a fondue pot's burner is ideal. As soon as the stock boils, put in your first vegetables, raise the heat and stir round. Cook quickly, adding the rest of the vegetables in order; the moment they are just tender (they should still have a bite), lift them out with a slotted spoon into a nylon sieve held over the pot. Drain them by shaking them over the pot, and turn them lightly into a warmed served dish. Taste one strand, add extra salt and pepper if you need to, lift the vegetables lightly with a fork to let the seasoning slip under the surface, and serve them, with pats of chilled butter or a sauce if you wish.

Done this way, most vegetables should cook in 3–5 minutes. For instance, see our Chinese Leaf Chowder recipe on page 76.

Stir-Frying

This is much the same as brief-dipping, except that you use a *very little* oil in a large shallow pan instead of liquid in a deep one. As in brief-dipping, a large part of the craft of stir-frying lies in presenting the assorted raw vegetables beautifully on the table in the order in which they will go into the pan, and in choosing vivid colour mixtures for gaiety on the plates.

Like brief-dipping, only start cooking when your diners are assembled with warmed plates in front of them. Heat the oil in a large shallow pan, such as an electric frying pan or a wok or a fairly deep skillet on a burner, and put in the vegetables in the order your recipe suggests. Cook the vegetables for just long enough to tenderize them, then scoop them up with a broad perforated slice or slotted spoon, drain them over the pan, and transfer them to a serving dish or on to the plates.

COOKING PULSES

In the past, dried beans, peas and other pulses of all kinds needed long hours of soaking before they were fit to cook. Modern pulses are on the whole much more amenable. Some, such as red lentils and split peas, can be cooked with no pre-soaking at all, in much the same time as fresh vegetables. Others, such as black-eyed beans, only need to have boiling water poured over them and then to be left to stand for an hour, followed by 20–40 minutes gentle boiling.

The rest, notably soya beans, whole yellow Norwegian peas, and chick-peas, still need long soaking and simmering. However, soya beans in particular are well worth the time they take since they contain 61 per cent protein in a form usable by human beings; so they can, by themselves, replace meat with its average value of 67 per cent protein. For general soaking and cooking times see the table on page 70.

Whatever kind of pulses you buy, try to get them from a busy supplier with a quick turnover because last year's old stock will take a long time to cook and will taste 'dead'. If you buy from loose or bulk-packed stock, always wash the pulses in a colander because they are likely to be dusty, or have small stones among them. Pick them over, then soak them, if they need it, in a really big bowl, with plenty of water. Refrigerate soya beans while soaking them because they ferment easily.

Cook your pulses in the water used for soaking them because it now contains some of their vitamins and flavour; do not add salt until after cooking as it toughens the skins. *Unlike* all other vegetables, cook pulses well in advance of when you want them because every batch will be slightly different and may need a different cooking time. Test the pulses by tasting at ten-minute intervals for the last half-hour of their cooking time. Pulses should reheat perfectly if you drain them well, and keep them covered and chilled while they wait.

The cooking time is, of course, much shorter if the pulses are cooked in a pressure cooker, shorter still if they are ground to flour or meal first. A fairly new development is the increasing supply of ready-ground meal and flour from pulses, nuts and grains—a form of processing even whole-food addicts welcome. You can now buy quite easily, for instance, soya flour, carob powder, flaked and cracked wheat and barley meal.

Processed pulses are useful for many dishes, but the whole, nutty, beans, peas or lentils are more attractive to look at, and are crunchier to eat. If you have a few beans left over after measuring a needed quantity, gather up several 'odd lots' and try cooking and serving a Bean Medley. Children, in particular, may like to experiment too, with growing bean sprouts from mung beans for salads. There is a lot more to using pulses nowadays than the pease pudding or boiled butter beans of thirty years ago.

SOAKING AND COOKING TIMES FOR PULSES

If your beans are young and in good condition, they should respond to being cooked as follows:

Name of bean	Soaking time (if water is added lukewarm)	Cooking time in soaking water	
		simmered	pressure cooked
aduki	6 hours or overnight	1½–2 hours	50 minutes
black-eyed	2–4 hours	1½–2 hours	35 minutes
butter	overnight	2–2½ hours	50 minutes
haricot	overnight	1½–2 hours	45 minutes
mung	2–4 hours	20 minutes	10 minutes
pinto	2–4 hours	1½ hours	35 minutes
red kidney	4 hours or overnight	1½–2 hours	50 minutes
soya	overnight	3–3½ hours +	2 hours +
and for good measure:			
chick-peas	overnight	3½–4 hours	2 hours +
split yellow or green peas	–	1½ hours	40 minutes
whole dried peas	4 hours	1½ hours	40 minutes
brown lentils	4 hours	1 hour	35 minutes
red lentils	–	30–40 minutes	–

Note: If you have a pressure cooker, always pressure cook beans and similar pulses (except red lentils). They not only cook faster, they look and taste better.

PREPARING AND USING FRUIT

The pleasure of eating fresh fruit, and the fact that most fruits *can* be eaten raw, means that you seldom need, or should want, to cook them. Apart from this, there is really no difference between fruit and vegetables, either in preparing them or in the uses to which you put them. Some 'vegetables' are in fact fruits, and some make good sweet dishes; while fruits such as apples, peaches and cherries can be used to excellent effect as vegetables, in salads serving as savoury food, and as a garnish for savoury dishes. It is a pity that we do not use vegetables for desserts and fruits with savoury foods more often, since they 'mix and match' so well. We have given you a few examples of these unusual uses for fruit and vegetables in this book, but we hope that you will experiment and find more.

The only real difference between fruit and vegetables is that fruits are even less stable than most vegetables. Delicate fruits can shrivel or become flabby, and lose their fresh sharp flavour, within hours of being harvested. You should always, if possible, gather (if you grow your own) or buy fruit on the same day that you intend to use it.

When preparing fruits, follow the same general rules as for preparing vegetables; in short, do as little to them as you can, and do it as quickly as you can. Wash them more carefully than vegetables because most fruits have delicate skins. Do not skin or peel fruits if you can help it; their looks are much less important than their food value. If you really need to strip them—for instance if your family dislikes the slightly furry taste of apricot or peach skin—dip the fruit in near-boiling water for an instant, no more; the skin should then slip off easily. This is the technique to use for most stone fruits and tomatoes. It is also a good way to deal with oranges because the whole peel then strips off cleanly, with all the pith.

Keep in mind that some fruits discolour almost instantly on contact with air. Always dip or steep fruits such as apples, pears, peaches, apricots or avocados in lemon or orange juice, cider, wine or French dressing (for a salad) as soon as you expose a new surface.

Some fruits are tart and need sweetening for both savoury and sweet dishes, whether you will eat them raw or cooked. You can simply sprinkle raw fruits with a sweetening substance, or you can steep them in a sweetened liquid, using it like a marinade. Whichever you do, bear in mind that brown sugar or molasses will discolour (and flavour) the fruit. If you do not want to use white sugar, use light-coloured clear honey or light American corn syrup if you can get it.

Adding flavourings to fruit is seldom a problem because its

flavour is usually so good on its own. However, for variety and
also pleasure, do experiment with using fresh chopped herbs
with raw or cooked fruit. Fresh chopped mint is a well-known
flavouring for a number of fruits such as apples, oranges, grapefruit and melon. Try fresh thyme or marjoram leaves with apples,
pears, or gooseberries; one or two finely chopped coriander
leaves with plums; rosemary with stone fruits; marjoram or
lemon balm with strawberries.

Even quite tough fruits will soften to some extent just by
steeping, but if you want to soften them by cooking yet want
them to keep their shape, poach them in plenty of sweetened
liquid. Use a good deal more liquid than when cooking vegetables in stock. Instead of stock, you will have a fruit syrup which
you can use again for steeping other fruit, or use as the basis of a
sauce, jelly for dessert or a sweet drink. However, make sure
that you only poach or gently simmer the fruit; never boil it.

Vegetables as Side Dishes

GLAZED BROCCOLI

Serve this side dish on a separate small plate because it both
tastes distinctive and looks so well dressed on its own; or use it as
a small vegetable dish with a poached-egg supper on a tray.

For each side-dish helping, use:

> 1 large or 2 medium broccoli spears
> 1 small onion, about 2 oz (50 g)
> ½ stick celery
> ¼ pint (125 ml) chicken or vegetable stock (page 135)
> a few drops of gravy browning if needed
> 3–4 small strips of sweet red pepper

Cut the stems off the broccoli to within 1 inch (2.5 cm) of the
flowers. Slice the onion. Slice the celery. Put the vegetables in a
small saucepan with the stock and a few drops of gravy browning
if it is pale; you want a rich-coloured glaze. Bring to the boil, half
cover the pan, and lower the heat to simmering point. Cook for
15–20 minutes until the broccoli and celery are just tender. You

can add a little extra stock while cooking, but only if you need to prevent it drying out. At the end of the cooking time, it should be reduced to a syrupy glaze.

While cooking the vegetables, cut a few shreds from a sweet red pepper. Add them to the saucepan about 5 minutes before the end of the cooking time.

The vegetables should not need any extra seasoning if the stock is well flavoured. Simply turn them on to a well-warmed small plate. Arrange the broccoli flowers close together, with the onion, celery and glaze over them. Top them with the shreds of pepper for their added crisp bite and colour.

BAKED LETTUCE

For 4 side-dish helpings, use:

    1 large firm Webb's lettuce
    salt and pepper
    2 teaspoons (2 × 5 ml spoon) dried marjoram or oregano
    4 spring onions, green and white parts
    2 tablespoons (2 × 15 ml spoons) finely diced cucumber
    4 tablespoons (4 × 15 ml spoons) tomato juice
    1 teaspoon (1 × 5 ml spoon) Worcester sauce

Remove any wilted or damaged outside lettuce leaves. Wash the lettuce well without breaking it apart. Cut off the root, and cut the lettuce into four quarters lengthways Lay each segment on a piece of foil large enough to enclose it completely. Sprinkle with salt and pepper and the herbs. Trim the spring onions. Chop the green parts over the lettuce. Halve the bulbs, and lay them on the lettuce with the cucumber. Mix together the tomato juice and Worcester sauce. Turn up the edges of the foil so that the sauce cannot run off, and pour the sauce mixture over the lettuce. Wrap each segment of lettuce completely in its foil sheath. Bake at 325°F (160°C) Gas 3 for 20 minutes. Unwrap and use as a side vegetable dish.

RADISHES WITH SPROUTS

For a quick dish to make after a busy day, use frozen sprouts and 2 chicken or vegetable stock cubes with about half the usual quantity of water. Black radishes can be kept in a vegetable rack for several days like carrots or turnips.

For 4 side-dish helpings, use:

> 12 oz (300 g) prepared fresh Brussels sprouts or frozen
>   sprouts
> 3 black radishes, about 5 oz (125 g) each
> 1 small onion, about 2 oz (50 g)
> ¾ pint (375 ml) strong chicken or vegetable stock (page 135) or
>   2 stock cubes and ¾ pint (375 ml) water (see recipe)
> salt and pepper if needed

Use frozen sprouts without thawing them. They will taste better
and will still take only about half as long to cook as fresh sprouts.

Wipe, then top and tail the radishes, but do not peel them; they
do not stain like salsify. Cut them into ½-inch (1 cm) cubes. Slice
the onion thinly.

Put the stock or crumbled cubes and water in a fair-sized
saucepan. Bring to the boil, then put in the sprouts, fresh or
frozen. Bring back to the boil, half cover, and cook frozen sprouts
for 2 minutes, fresh sprouts for 8–12 minutes, depending on size.
Add the cubed radishes, then strew the onion on top. Half cover
again, bring back to the boil, and cook for 6–10 minutes longer
until all the vegetables are tender. Drain, taste, and add a little
salt and pepper if needed; or boil down any remaining stock until
syrupy, then pour it over the vegetables.

HOT CURRIED SALAD

For 4 side-dish helpings, use:

> 2 young carrots about 2 oz (50 g) each
> 6 large radishes
> 6 medium spring onions, green and white parts
> ½ small sweet green pepper if you wish
> 1 × 4 inch (1 × 10 cm) piece cucumber
> ¼ pint (125 ml) vegetable stock (page 135) and tomato juice
>   mixed, or Tomato Cocktail Sauce (page 139)
> ½ teaspoon (1 × 2.5 ml spoon) garam masala
> ½ small sharp apple, about 2 oz (50 g)
> salt if needed

Slice the carrots very thinly, or grate them coarsely. Slice the
radishes thickly. Cut the spring onions, both green and white
parts, into ½-inch (1 cm) pieces. Cut the pepper flesh, if using,

into ½-inch (1 cm) squares, and the cucumber into ½-inch (1 cm) cubes.

Heat the liquid in a saucepan. When it reaches simmering point, put in the carrot, radish and pepper. Sprinkle with the garam masala, and simmer for 5 minutes. Add the spring onions, and simmer for another 4–7 minutes, until the carrot is beginning to soften and the radish skins are pale. While simmering, core and dice the apple. Add the cucumber and apple to the salad and simmer for another 2–3 minutes. Taste the sauce (which should be reduced almost to a glaze), and adapt the seasoning if you wish. Serve hot, with any sauce still remaining.

Note: Do not overcook the salad. The vegetables should still have a bite.

SPINACH WITH APPLE

For 4 side-dish helpings, use:

    1 lb (450 g) fresh spinach
    1 medium sharp dessert apple
    2 large spring onions
    2 tablespoons (2 × 15 ml spoons) lemon juice
    salt and pepper

Cut the stalks off the spinach. Coarsely shred the leaves.

Quarter and core the apple, then dice it. Chop both the green and white parts of the spring onion. Put both in a large saucepan with the lemon juice. Simmer them, covered, for 3 minutes. Add the spinach, plenty of salt and pepper, and 3 tablespoons (3 × 15 ml spoons) water. Cover and simmer for 8–10 minutes until the spinach is just tender. Toss all together, and serve piled on a plate.

Main-Course Vegetable Dishes

CHINESE LEAF CHOWDER

Offer the chowder as a soupy stew with Soya Rolls (page 29); or drain off most of the stock, and serve the vegetables with pasta or Polenta (page 22). In this case, you can thicken the liquid for a sauce.

For 4–6 main-course helpings, use:

> about 13 oz (350 g) Chinese leaves
> ½ pint (250 ml) vegetable stock (page 135)
> 2 onions, about 3 oz (75 g) each
> 2 tomatoes, about 2½ oz (75 g) each
> 2 tablespoons (2 × 15 ml spoons) salted peanuts
> 1 tablespoon (1 × 15 ml spoon) smooth peanut butter
> pepper
> a few grains of chilli powder

Finely shred the leaves, especially any stems. Put the stock in a large saucepan, and pack in the leaves. Cover securely. Bring to the boil and cook for 3 minutes. Take the pan off the heat. Do not uncover it yet.

Finely chop the onions with the tomatoes. Crush the peanuts into fragments. Uncover the pan, and add these ingredients to it with the peanut butter. Stir over gentle heat for 5–8 minutes, until the onions are just tender. Season well but carefully. Serve very hot.

CASSEROLED GREEN LEEKS

Many people throw away the green parts of leeks but these coarser parts can make an interesting, and certainly an economical, dish. So why waste good greenstuff by throwing them away?

Try instead this easily cooked 'bake' with its sweet-sour fruit stimulus. If you like, increase its protein value by adding some cooked soya or mung beans for the last 15 minutes of its cooking time.

For 4 main-course helpings, use:

> green tops of 4 large leeks
> 1 large or 2 medium onions

1 large or 2 small sour cooking apples
juice of ½ lemon
1 oz (25 g) margarine
grated rind of ½ lemon
2 tablespoons (2 × 15 ml spoons) molasses
2 tablespoons (2 × 15 ml spoons) cider vinegar
salt

Discard any withered leaves and wash the leek-tops thoroughly.
Remove the extreme tips, and cut the rest in thin slices. Chop the
onion. Core and cube the apple, and toss at once in the lemon
juice. Melt the margarine in the bottom of a flameproof casserole
which will hold all the ingredients, and sauté the onion in it until
just golden. Add all the other ingredients including any lemon
juice with the apple. Cover the casserole closely, and put it over
low heat until the mixture hisses. Transfer it to the oven, heated
to 350°F (180°C) Gas 4, and bake for 45–55 minutes or until the
leek leaves are very tender. Taste and add extra salt if you wish.
Serve very hot, with Herb Pudding (page 89).

POOR MAN'S GOOSE

For 4–6 main-course helpings, use:

1 medium marrow, about 2¼–2½ lb (1–1.1 kg)
4 oz (100 g) margarine
1 large onion
1 stick celery
4 oz (100 g) cracked wheat
¼ pint (125 ml) strong vegetable stock (page 135)
¼ pint (125 ml) dry still cider or apple juice
salt and pepper
6–8 sage leaves
1 cooking apple, about 6 oz (150 g)
2 oz (50 g) seedless raisins
extra margarine for greasing
apple sauce

Split the marrow lengthways, take out the seeds and spread the
hollows with a little of the margarine. Chop the onion with the
celery, very finely. Melt 2 oz (50 g) of the remaining margarine in
a large deep frying pan or skillet, and fry the onion and celery
until soft but not coloured. Add the cracked wheat, stock and

cider or juice with a little seasoning. Bring gently to simmering point, cover, and simmer for 15 minutes. While simmering, finely chop the sage leaves, and chop the apple. When the cracked-wheat mixture is ready, mix in the sage, apple and raisins. Leave to stand until cool enough to handle.

Fill one or both marrow halves with the mixture. If you only fill one, you will have less stuffing in the 'goose' and can serve forcemeat balls with it (half the stuffing will make 8–10 balls), or you can keep the empty marrow half for a different stuffed dish. (If you stuff both, you can either re-shape the marrow as a whole or bake the two halves separately, as you wish.)

Put the re-shaped marrow, or one or both halves (cut side up), in a baking tin. Roll any remaining stuffing into forcemeat balls. Put the forcemeat balls into the baking tin with the marrow. Dot the tops of the marrow halves (or the top skin if re-shaped) with a little more margarine. Put any remaining margarine in the tin.

Cover the marrow loosely with greased foil, and bake it at 375°F (190°C) Gas 5 for 1–1½ hours, depending on its size; it should be tender but not squashy. Baste both the marrow and any force-meat balls two or three times, while baking, with the margarine in the tin. Uncover the marrow 15 minutes before the end of the cooking time, baste well, and let it finish cooking uncovered.

Put the marrow on a heated serving plate with any forcemeat balls. Serve it with apple sauce.

BAKED DINNER POTATOES

This way of stuffing potatoes saves you having to handle them when they are hot, yet lets you serve them freshly baked.

Use the potato hollowed out of the centres to make Vegetable Cream Sauce, page 139.

For 4 main-course helpings, use:

> 4 baking potatoes, about 10 oz (250 g) each
> 4 oz (100 g) full-fat soft cheese
> 2 dessertspoons (2 × 10 ml spoons) milk
> 1 oz (25 g) Swiss Gruyère cheese
> 1 stick celery
> 1 dessertspoon (1 × 10 ml spoon) natural wheat bran
> ½ teaspoon (1 × 2.5 ml spoon) teaspoon dried marjoram
> salt and pepper
> margarine for greasing

Scrub the potatoes and rub them dry without breaking the skins. Beat the soft cheese until light, then beat in the milk slowly to make a smooth cream. Grate and add the Gruyère cheese. Shred the celery and mix it into the cheeses with the bran, herb and seasoning. Cut a sliver off the top of each potato, and use a spoon to dig out enough of the centre to hold a quarter of the cheese mixture. Fill the cheese mixture into the hollowed potatoes. Grease four squares of foil large enough to wrap round the potatoes. Put one potato in the centre of each foil square. Twist the edges of the foil over it, to enclose it completely without touching the cheese topping. Put the foil parcels on a greased baking sheet, and bake the potatoes at 350°F (180°C) Gas 4 for 45 minutes–1 hour, or until the potatoes are tender when pierced with a thin skewer through the foil.

To serve, just open the foil packages, turn back the foil and expose the creamy cheese surface. Eat with spoons.

Cereals and Pulses

COOKING PASTA (Basic recipe)

Any pasta, no matter what shape it is, is cooked in plain boiling salted water. The only change is that, for some dishes, the pasta is drained when only partly cooked and finishes cooking in the oven.

For each main-course helping of pasta served just with a sauce, use:

about 4 oz (100 g) dry pasta
2 pints (1.1 litres) cold water
1 teaspoon (1 × 5 ml spoon) salt

Break or cut long rods of pasta into about 6-inch (15 cm) lengths. Bring the water to a fast boil, then add the salt to it. Push long pasta down into the water, a little at a time so that it does not go off the boil; drop round or flat pasta shapes into the water a few at a time. Boil the pasta, uncovered, until it has lost any taste of raw flour, but is still firm to bite (what Italians call *'al dente'*). It must *not* be mushy.

Test whether the pasta is ready 2 minutes before you think it ought to be. Take out one strand or shape and taste it. If it is not yet ready, test it again every 2 minutes until it is done.

Short or very thin strands (e.g. vermicelli) or small round shapes should be fully cooked in 5–8 minutes, long flat ribbons and thin strands in 7–10 minutes, large wide strands and long tubes (such as macaroni) in 10–15 minutes.

Buckwheat pasta takes about the same time as standard white pasta. Wholemeal pasta may take 2–3 minutes longer.

If you want to finish the cooking in the oven, cook any pasta for 5 minutes only.

Drain fully cooked pasta in a large colander. Then return it to the dry pan and put it on the side of the stove near the heat for 2–3 minutes, or until you are ready to complete your dish. If it has to wait more than 5 minutes, put it in a sieve lined with a damp cloth, and place the sieve over a pan of hot water; cover the pasta with buttered paper. If you are going to finish the cooking in the oven, lay the pasta pieces side by side on a damp cloth, not touching each other.

Prepare the sauce you wish to use, then lay the pasta in your serving or baking dish, adding the sauce as the recipe directs.

PASTA WITH MUSHROOM SAUCE

The sauce can be served over rice or pasta; it is equally good with either, and is quick and easy to make.

For 4 main-course helpings, use:

   1 lb (450 g) wholemeal pasta
   1 small onion
   $\frac{1}{2}$ clove garlic
   10 oz (250 g) small flat mushrooms
   1 tablespoon (1 × 15 ml spoon) butter or margarine
   1 tablespoon (1 × 15 ml spoon) cooking oil
   2 teaspoons (2 × 5 ml spoons) chopped parsley
   81% extraction flour for sprinkling
   4–6 tablespoons (4–6 × 15 ml spoons) vegetable stock (page 135)
   salt and pepper
   a knob of butter

Cook the pasta as described above until no floury taste remains. While cooking it, finely chop the onion and garlic, and thinly slice the mushrooms. Heat the fat and oil in a fairly large frying pan, and sauté the onion, garlic and parsley until soft. Sprinkle them well with flour, then stir in the sliced mushrooms, stock and seasoning. Simmer until the mushrooms are soft. They will give off enough liquid to make a slightly thickened sauce with the flour.

Drain the pasta and pile it on a heated serving dish. Mix a knob of butter into the mushroom sauce, and serve it over the pasta.

COOKING BROWN RICE (Basic recipe)

Brown rice is a food which contains most nutrients the human body needs; far more than the same quantity of white rice, which is polished to remove the husk.

You can get long- and short-grain brown rice and also a sweet rice which is slightly more glutinous when cooked.

Cooked brown rice keeps well for 4–5 days in a refrigerator or for at least 4 days in a larder; so you may find it worth while to cook a fairly large quantity at a time, to use during the following week.

For 4–6 main-course 'carrier' helpings, use:

8–10 oz (200–250 g) brown rice
¾ pint (375 ml) water
½ teaspoon (1 × 2.5 ml spoon) salt

Rinse the rice lightly in a strainer under cold running water. Put it into a pan with the water and salt, and bring slowly to the boil. Lower the heat and simmer gently with a lid on the pan for about 25 minutes. Do not stir. Check whether the pan is dry; if so, add a little more water. Ten minutes later, check again, and add a little more water if necessary. Repeat after another 5-minute interval. The rice should be cooked in about 40 minutes. When done, it should be tender but still have a bite and the grains should still be intact. The pan should be dry or very nearly dry, and the rice should just be beginning to stick to the bottom.

Remove the pan from the stove and let it stand, covered, for 5–10 minutes before use.

Note: If you have a pressure cooker, always use it to cook brown rice. All the water is absorbed cleanly and the rice grains stay separate. Allow 5 minutes after bringing to pressure.

ALL'ONDA RISOTTO

For 4–6 main-course helpings, use:

    2 pints (1.1. litres) vegetable stock (page 135)
    1 small onion
    1 oz (25 g) button mushrooms
    2 oz (50 g) butter or margarine
    12 oz (300 g) brown rice
    1 teaspoon (1 × 5 ml spoon) tomato purée
    2 tablespoons (2 × 15 ml spoons) shelled young peas
    2 tablespoons (2 × 15 ml spoons) seedless raisins
    2 tablespoons (2 × 15 ml spoons) chopped canned pimiento
    2 teaspoons (2 × 5 ml spoons) chopped fresh thyme, or
        marjoram leaves or 1 teaspoon (1 × 5 ml spoon) dried
        thyme or marjoram
    salt and pepper
    3 tablespoons (3 × 15 ml spoons) natural yoghurt
    grated Parmesan cheese if you wish

Warm the stock, and set it aside. Chop the onion and mushrooms; keep them separate. In a large deep frying pan or skillet,
fry the onion in 1 oz (25 g) of the fat until soft but not coloured.
Add the rice and purée, and stir them in until the rice is well
coated. Then mix in the mushrooms, peas, raisins, pimiento and
herbs with about ¼ pint (125 ml) of the stock. Let the rice absorb all
the liquid. Then add ¾ pint (375 ml) more stock, little by little,
letting the rice absorb the liquid each time before adding more.
Add the remaining stock, season well, and cook gently until the
rice is tender and most of the liquid is absorbed. It will take 40–45
minutes in all.

Stir in the rest of the fat and the yoghurt off the heat. Taste and
adapt the seasoning if you wish. Serve while the rice is still
glistening, with the few spoonfuls of simmering liquid still in the
pan.

For a piquant flavour, serve a bowl of grated Parmesan cheese
with the risotto.

MEXICAN BEANS

Beans in some form are a staple dish all over Mexico and in parts of the south-western United States.

For 6–8 side-dish helpings, use:

12–14 oz (350–375 g) red kidney beans
2 pints (1.1. litres) water
salt
4 oz (100 g) bacon fat or margarine
pepper or chilli powder if you wish
dried marjoram or oregano if you wish

Soak and cook the beans as in the table on page 70. Cook them until the skins wrinkle and break, a little longer than usual if necessary. Add a little more boiling water while cooking, if needed. Stir gently from time to time. About 30 minutes before the end of the cooking time, add salt to suit your taste. When the beans are cooked, drain them, but keep any cooking liquid.

Melt the fat in a large deep frying pan or skillet. Put in a few tablespoonfuls (15 ml spoonfuls) of beans and mash them down into the fat until fairly smooth. Add gradually, and stir in, enough bean cooking liquid or water to make a thick gravy or sauce. Stir it until it thickens. (You can make as much or as little sauce as you like, depending on how many beans you mash into the fat and how much liquid you add. You can also flavour the sauce with extra salt, and with pepper and dried marjoram or oregano if you wish.) Pour the hot sauce over the beans, reheat them if they need it, and serve very hot.

CONGRIS

Rice and bean mixtures are used a great deal in all parts of the West Indies. With small additions, you can make this one into a good main-course meal for 4 people.

For 6 side-dish helpings, use:

1 sweet green pepper
2 medium tomatoes
1 medium onion
1 clove garlic

1 oz (25 g) bacon fat or 2 tablespoons (2 × 15 ml spoons)
   ground-nut oil
salt and pepper
4 oz (100 g) brown rice
¾ pint (375 ml) water
8 oz (200 g) cooked red kidney beans
1 tablespoon (1 × 15 ml spoon) desiccated coconut if you
   wish

Seed and chop the pepper, quarter and chop the tomato. Chop
the onion and squeeze the garlic over it. Heat the fat or oil in a
heavy saucepan, and fry the onion and garlic gently until soft.
Stir in the pepper and tomatoes, and season well. Add the rice
and water. Cover the pan and simmer for 20 minutes. Add the
beans and continue cooking for another 15–20 minutes, until the
rice is fully cooked and has absorbed most of the liquid. Stir in the
coconut if you use it, and serve while still hot.

COOKING SOYA BEANS

Soya beans contain more protein than any other bean so they are
well worth the extra care and long cooking they need. Soak them
overnight in enough fresh water to cover them like other beans
but keep them in a cool place because they can ferment easily.
Top up the water once or twice. Soya beans swell more than
most, often to three times their original size; so make sure you
have a large enough pan, both for soaking and cooking them.

   To cook them, add enough extra water to cover the beans if
needed, half cover the pan, and bring it gently to the boil. Lower
the heat, and simmer the beans for 3–3½ hours, topping up with
more boiling water occasionally, and stirring gently when you do
so. The beans are cooked when swollen, shiny and tender;
undercooked beans taste raw and can give you indigestion. Season the cooked beans with salt and pepper. Drain off any free
water for cooking other vegetables, and mix a little fat and a few
chopped fresh herbs or ground spices with the beans.

   Since soya beans take so long to cook, yet are so valuable, it is
well worth while cooking them in quantity and freezing a stock of
them if you can.

SOYA SAUSAGES

For 4 main-course helpings, use:

    1 large clove garlic
    1 medium onion
    4 tablespoons (4 × 15 ml spoons) margarine
    8 oz (200 g) cooked soya beans
    3 tablespoons (3 × 15 ml spoons) cooked brown or red
        lentils
    4 tablespoons (4 × 15 ml spoons) white flour
    ½ pint (250 ml) warm milk
    2 teaspoons (2 × 5 ml spoons) dried basil
    2 tablespoons (2 × 15 ml spoons) chopped parsley
    a good pinch of ground coriander
    salt and pepper
    2 eggs
    dried wholemeal breadcrumbs for coating
    extra margarine as needed

Finely chop the garlic and onion. Melt 2 tablespoons (2 × 15 ml spoons) of the margarine in a small frying pan, and cook them until soft; do not colour them. Pound them with the soya beans and lentils until they are well blended and fairly smooth.

Melt the rest of the margarine in a small saucepan, stir in the white flour and cook them together for 2–3 minutes. Stir in the milk gradually, and cook gently, still stirring, until the panada is very thick. Leave until cool enough to handle. Mix together the bean and lentil paste, panada, herbs, coriander, salt and pepper. Beat one egg until liquid and mix it in. Refrigerate the mixture for at least 30 minutes.

Beat the second egg. With floured hands, shape the bean mixture into 8 cork shapes. Dip the 'sausages' in the egg, then roll in breadcrumbs. Repeat the coatings to make a firm outside crust.

Grease a shallow baking tin. Put in the 'sausages'. Dot them with a little extra fat. Then bake them at 425°F (220°C) Gas 7 for about 20 minutes or until the crusts are firm and golden.

Serve them very hot with Tomato Cocktail Sauce (page 139) and with a green vegetable.

CORN AND NUT CRUMBLE

If you keep frozen soya beans in stock, this is a useful store-cupboard supper dish for times when you cannot shop. If you can add finely shredded green leaf vegetables such as Chinese leaves, so much the better.

For 2–3 helpings, use:

>   1 × 7 oz (1 × 198 g) can whole kernel sweet corn
>   1 × 8 oz (1 × 226 g) can tomatoes
>   ½ small carrot, about 1 oz (25 g)
>   4 oz (100 g) cooked soya beans
>   ½ teaspoon (1 × 2.5 ml spoon) salt
>   ¼·teaspoon (½ × 2.5 ml spoon) pepper
>   1 teaspoon (1 × 5 ml spoon) dried basil, savory or mixed herbs
>   a good pinch of paprika
>   1 teaspoon (1 × 5 ml spoon) muscovado sugar
>   1 dessertspoon (1 × 10 ml spoon) grated onion
>   1 oz (25 g) salted peanuts
>   1 oz (25 g) dark brown rye breadcrumbs
>   margarine as needed

Drain the sweet corn and tomatoes. Grate the carrot. Mix together all the ingredients except the peanuts, breadcrumbs and margarine. Grease a 1¼-pint (700 ml) pie dish with margarine, and spread the mixture in it, in an even layer. Grate or grind the peanuts, not too finely, and mix them with the breadcrumbs. Sprinkle them over the dish. Flake extra margarine over the crumble. Bake the dish at 350°F (180°C) Gas 4 for 25–30 minutes. Serve hot from the dish.

TEXTURED VEGETABLE PROTEIN

Dry TVP, as it is often called,.is a useful standby to have on the store-cupboard shelf. Wholly stable yet quick to make up, it can 'extend' meat or make a vegetable dish into a full-scale protein meal. One can buy it in several different forms such as chunks or mince, and in several flavours. Most types just need soaking or simmering for a short time in stock or water to make them swell and be ready for cooking with other foods. The cooking instructions are given on the manufacturer's packet, and should be followed closely.

ITALIAN SUNSET STEW

For 4 main-course helpings, use:

2 onions, about 3 oz (75 g) each
1 lb (450 g) tomatoes
½ sweet red pepper
1 tablespoon (1 × 15 ml spoon) vegetable cooking oil
4 oz (100 g) prepared textured vegetable protein or cooked soya beans
1 oz (25 g) tomato purée
1 dessertspoon (1 × 10 ml spoon) dried basil
a few grains of chilli powder
½ pint (250 ml) water
12 oz (300 g) wholewheat spaghetti
1 tablespoon (1 × 15 ml spoon) cornflour if you wish
1 tablespoon (1 × 15 ml spoon) water if using cornflour
salt and pepper

Chop the onions and tomatoes. Finely chop the pepper. Heat the oil in a large frying pan, and fry the onions until they are soft and light gold. Add the tomatoes, pepper, the textured vegetable protein or beans, and the tomato purée. Stir in the basil and chilli powder, and add the water. Simmer gently for 15 minutes with the pan half covered.

While simmering, cook the spaghetti in fast-boiling, lightly salted water for 10–12 minutes.

If you wish to have a thick sauce, blend the cornflour and water to a smooth paste, and stir it into the frying pan at the end of the 15 minutes' cooking time. Simmer for 3 minutes, stirring the whole time. Season the sauce well.

Drain the spaghetti and pile it in the centre of a warmed serving dish. Surround it with the thick, rich tomato mixture. Serve it at once, while still really hot.

COOKING MAIZE AND OTHER GRAIN MEAL

Cooking oatmeal in liquid is covered in the recipe for Oatmeal Porridge on page 21. Cooking maize meal in liquid is covered on page 22 in the recipe for Polenta; semolina is cooked in the same way. Grain meal can be either baked or cooked as in the recipes which follow.

BAKED MAIZE (SPOON BREAD)

You can serve this moist dish instead of potatoes or a pulse. In America, it is traditionally served with Southern Fried Chicken, but it is equally good with roast pork or duck, and with ham. It is also good with a spicy sauce or vegetable stew. Serve it with plenty of butter.

For 6 side-dish helpings, use:

> ¾ pint (375 ml) milk
> 4 oz (100 g) maize meal (corn meal, polenta) or semolina
> 2 tablespoons (2 × 15 ml spoons) butter or margarine
> butter or margarine for greasing
> 3 eggs
> 1 teaspoon (1 × 5 ml spoon) salt
> ½ teaspoon (1 × 2.5 ml spoon) baking powder

Put the milk in a fairly large saucepan and bring it to scalding point. Sprinkle in the maize meal or semolina gradually, and stir over gentle heat until the mixture is very thick. Take the pan off the heat. Melt the fat and stir it in, then let the mixture cool a little.

Grease a 3-pint (1.7 litre) pie dish or oven-to-table baking dish. Separate the eggs. Beat the egg yolks with the salt until light. Stir them into the maize mixture. Beat the egg whites with the baking powder until stiff. With a pliable rubber scraper or whisk, fold them into the maize mixture. Turn the mixture gently into the greased dish, and bake at 350°F (180°C) Gas 4 for 40 minutes or until the maize is golden on top. Serve at once, from the dish, with a generous spoonful of butter on each helping.

SAVOURY POLENTA CAKES

Make these 'cakes' as a change from soft Baked Maize, to serve instead of potatoes, pasta or rice.

For 6 side-dish helpings, use:

> 1½ pints (850 ml) water
> 1 teaspoon (1 × 5 ml spoon) salt
> 8 oz (200 g) polenta (corn meal, maize meal)
> 1 dessertspoon (1 × 10 ml spoon) dried mixed herbs
> margarine as needed

1 tablespoon (1 × 15 ml spoon) chopped parsley
pepper
a few grains of cayenne pepper or chilli powder

Bring the lightly salted water to the boil in a large pan. Sprinkle in the polenta and dried herbs, stirring all the time. Lower the heat until the water only just simmers. Cover the pan, put it on an asbestos mat, and simmer very gently for 25 minutes. Stir from time to time while cooking.

Grease an 11 × 8 inch (27 × 20 cm) baking tray with margarine. When the polenta is ready, stir in the parsley and seasonings, and turn the mixture into the tray. Smooth the surface. Cover the polenta loosely with greased paper, and leave it until quite cold and firm. Then cut it into rounds with a 2½-inch (6.5 cm) cutter. Lift the rounds off the tray with a palette knife, and grill or fry them with a little fat, turning once, until both sides are lightly browned with a crisp surface. They take 7–10 minutes to grill, about 5 minutes to fry.

HERB PUDDING

This is a very old traditional savoury pudding, originally made with steeped groats and boiled in a cloth. It was served before or with meat, to take the edge off the appetite, and it gave new interest to spring meals after the plain suet puddings eaten all winter.

For 6 side-dish helpings, use:

4 oz (100 g) medium oatmeal
4 oz (100 g) wholemeal self-raising flour
4 oz (100 g) shredded suet
finely chopped young spinach leaves or young turnip greens, parsley and green and white spring onion, about 2 oz (50 g) weight in all
2 teaspoons (2 × 5 ml spoons) finely chopped fresh thyme or lovage
salt

Mix all the ingredients well, and moisten with cold water to make a stiff dough. Turn the mixture into a well-greased 1¾-pint (1 litre) pudding basin, leaving at least 1 inch (2.5 cm) headspace. Cover securely. Put a cloth in the bottom of a large pan, fill the pan about a third full of water and bring to the boil. Put in the basin (the water should come half-way up the sides) and half-steam for 3 hours. Top up the pan with extra boiling water when necessary. Serve the pudding from the basin or leave to stand at room temperature for 7–10 minutes, then turn out.

Like Baked Maize or Savoury Polenta Cakes, above, use the pudding instead of potatoes with any plainly cooked meat, moistened with gravy or the pan-juices from a roast. It is also good sliced and fried.

LOUTH OATIES

For 24–28 oaties, use:

> 1 lb (450 g) mashed potatoes
> 6 oz (150 g) fine oatmeal or as needed (see recipe)
> 1 tablespoon (1 × 15 ml spoon) grated onion if you wish
> salt and pepper
> a little milk if needed
> dripping or margarine for greasing

Mix the potatoes, oatmeal, onion, if used, and seasoning together, to make a fairly stiff dough. You may need extra oatmeal if the potatoes are wet or a little milk if the oatmeal is floury. Roll out about ¼ inch (5 mm) thick on a floured surface. Cut into triangles or rounds, and prick each one with a fork. Cook on a well-greased griddle or heavy frying pan for about 10 minutes, turning once to brown and crisp both sides. Serve hot with plenty of butter instead of potatoes, for instance with poached smoked haddock or with baked (or grilled) tomatoes.

SALADS OF ALL SORTS

MAKING SALADS

Mixed salads, in particular, can be varied unendingly in their ingredients and colours, according to the way you arrange them and the dressing you choose. However, here are a few general guidelines to help you make any salad a good one of its kind.

1. Your saladings (to use a pleasant old term) must be as fresh as you can get them and preferably in season locally, when they will have peak flavour.
2. Choose saladings with contrasting colours, and with flavours which will remain distinct yet combine well.
3. Do not choose too many different ingredients for a mixed salad; their flavours may fight, and a dressing which suits one may not suit them all.
4. Allow plenty of time for salad-making. It takes time to cut up vegetables and fruit and arrange them decoratively.
5. Do not chop any salad ingredients too finely, especially for mixed salads. Their flavours will be lost, and soft or watery saladings may go mushy.
6. Keep all saladings as crisp as possible. Only rinse or wash them briefly. If you cook vegetables for a salad, drain and dry them really well. Always drain salad (and other) vegetables and fruit in a nylon sieve; metal discolours them, and gives them its own flavour.
7. Remember the gorgeously decorative effect of *not* mixing the saladings in a mixed salad. For instance, alternate rows of orange carrot, green peas, snowy and yellow hard-boiled egg look dramatic on a platter. Only, on the colour front, beware of beetroot. Unless you want to make a pink salad like our Pink Celeriac Salad on page 96, serve it on its own, just mixed with grated onion and seasoned. (The same goes for pickled walnuts.)
8. Do not dress a salad until the last moment. Nothing is nastier than soggy salad. We like to offer the dressing ingredients for

most plain salads separately, and let each person dress his own
in a small bowl.

9. Serve almost all salads slightly colder than normal room temperature. Chill in hot weather, but not for long; otherwise put
them in a cool place such as a larder. Either way, keep salads
covered until serving time; the best way is in a large plastic bag
which covers the salad loosely.

We confess that, in the salads which follow, we have not
always adhered to these guidelines. There can be, however, good
reasons for breaking the rules. For instance, a dressing intended
to bring out the flavour of particular ingredients may need to
blend with them before serving; in such cases, the salad should
be dressed ahead of time.

One more important point. We have suggested definite quantities in most of our salad recipes, but you may need to change
them slightly. Your cabbage for the Fruit Slaw (page 103), for
example, may have a lot of coarse outer leaves which, when
stripped off, leave you with rather less than 1 lb (450 g) cabbage.
You need not be too particular about such things in salad-
making, provided the proportions of the ingredients (in a mixed
salad) remain about the same.

Remember, however, that the number of helpings we have
suggested in each recipe assumes that the salad will be served as a
starter or a side salad, or that other salads will be served as well; it
may make a skimpy main course on its own.

SALAD DRESSINGS

Several salad dressings are 'built in' to the recipes in this section.
Use them with different salads, to vary them, if you feel so
inclined. We give other recipes for salad dressings below, and
you will find a recipe for Curried Mayonnaise on page 33.

FRENCH DRESSING

For about 8 fl oz (200 ml) dressing, use:

    2 fl oz (50 ml) white wine vinegar
    1 teaspoon (1 × 5 ml spoon) salt
    a good pinch of white pepper
    ½ teaspoon (1 × 2.5 ml spoon) dry mustard

a few drops of clear honey if you wish
a few grains of cayenne pepper
5–6 fl oz (125–150 ml) salad oil

Put the vinegar and seasonings in a jar with a secure stopper, and shake vigorously. Add the oil and shake again until fully blended. Taste and add extra seasoning or oil if you wish. Serve at room temperature, and shake well just before use.

FRENCH DRESSING WITH WALNUTS

Use 1 fl oz (25 ml) each cider vinegar and apple juice instead of wine vinegar, and slightly less seasoning than usual. Use fresh walnut oil if you can get it. Add 1 dessertspoon (1 × 10 ml spoon) finely chopped (not ground) walnuts.

ROQUEFORT SALAD DRESSING

Use only a pinch of salt, and no mustard. Add a few grains of ground mace, a little extra oil (if you wish), and 1–1½ oz (25–35 g) crumbled Roquefort or other blue cheese. For a smooth dressing, pound the cheese and seasonings, adding the vinegar and oil little by little, or process in an electric blender.

This dressing should keep well for 2–3 days if stored in the refrigerator in a securely stoppered jar.

APPLE JUICE SALAD DRESSING

One needs surprisingly little dressing to moisten a salad. The quantity given here will dress an average side salad for 3–4 people.

For about 2½ fl oz (65 ml) dressing, use:

1 tablespoon (1 × 15 ml spoon) cider vinegar
1 tablespoon apple juice (1 × 15 ml spoon) apple juice
salt and pepper
a pinch of dry mustard
½ teaspoon (1 × 2.5 ml spoon) clear honey
3 tablespoons (3 × 15 ml spoons) olive oil or good salad oil

Put all the ingredients into a screw-topped jar and shake it hard until they are completely blended. Taste and adapt the seasoning if you wish. Shake the bottle again just before dressing the salad.

GINGER SALAD DRESSING

For about 2½ fl oz (65 ml) dressing, use:

    2 tablespoons (2 × 15 ml spoons) soy sauce
    3 tablespoons (3 × 15 ml spoons) cider vinegar
    1 teaspoon (1 × 5 ml spoon) clear honey
    a good pinch of ground ginger
    2 tablespoons (2 × 15 ml spoons) salad oil if you wish

Mix all the ingredients except the oil in a bottle or jar with a secure
stopper. Close the container, and shake the bottle sharply to
blend them. Taste and add the oil if you wish. Re-stopper, and
shake again. Pour over the salad ingredients, and toss well.

YOGHURT SLAW DRESSING (Basic recipe)

This is enough dressing to coat ¼ medium-sized white cabbage or
slaw for 4 people.

For about 6 fl oz (150 ml) dressing, use:

    ½ clove garlic
    salt
    ¼ pint (125 ml) natural yoghurt
    1 teaspoon (1 × 5 ml spoon) home-made mustard (page
      138)
    1 tablespoon (1 × 15 ml spoon) lemon juice
    1 tablespoon (1 × 15 ml spoon) finely snipped chives or
      fresh thyme or sage leaves
    pepper

Skin the garlic, then crush it with salt, using a knife-blade.
Thoroughly mix together all the ingredients except salt and pepper. Taste, and add extra mustard and salt if needed, and (probably) a good grinding of pepper.

GOLDEN VALLEY MAYONNAISE

For about 6 fl oz (150 ml) dressing, use:

    1 tablespoon (1 × 15 ml spoon) natural yoghurt
    ¼ pint (125 ml) mayonnaise
    ¼ teaspoon (½ × 2.5 ml spoon) Worcester sauce
    ½ teaspoon (1 × 2.5 ml spoon) chopped parsley

½ teaspoon (1 × 2.5 ml spoon) chopped chives or spring
   onion green
1 dessertspoon (1 × 10 ml spoon) lemon juice
salt and pepper
a pinch of turmeric
a few drops of clear honey if you wish

Fold (do not stir) the yoghurt into the mayonnaise. Add the
Worcester sauce, herbs and lemon juice. Stir them in very gently.
Taste and season, adding enough turmeric to give the sauce a
creamy-yellow colour. Taste again, and add honey if you wish.
Use with white meats, especially chicken, or with a pasta salad.

CABBAGE SALAD

Try raw white cabbage with just an oil and vinegar dressing
instead of the usual creamy slaw. You will be surprised at how
good it is. Keep the soaking water for cooking other vegetables.
Try grated celeriac the same way.

For 4 first-course or side-dish helpings, use:

about 12 oz (300 g) young white cabbage
salt
¼ teaspoon (½ × 2.5 ml spoon) caraway seeds
2–3 dessertspoons (2–3 × 10 ml spoons) olive oil
1½ teaspoons (3 × 2.5 ml spoons) cider vinegar
paprika
pepper

Shred the cabbage very finely. Put it into iced, salted water for
about 1 hour. While it soaks, crush or grind the caraway seeds to
fragments.
   Drain the cabbage and dry it well in a soft cloth. Put it in a bowl
and mix in the seeds. Make a dressing with the oil, vinegar, and
just enough paprika, salt and pepper to give it a little spiciness.
Shake the dressing ingredients together in a securely stoppered
jar or bottle. Trickle enough dressing over the cabbage to moisten
it lightly. Serve the remaining dressing in a bottle with a secure
stopper, so that it can be shaken well just before use.

CARROT AND PEAR SALAD

For 4–6 first-course or side-dish helpings, use:

 ½ orange
 2 large firm pears, not too sweet
 grated rind and juice of 1 small lemon
 2 dessertspoons (2 × 10 ml spoons) clear honey
 3 carrots, about 3 oz (75 g) each
 1 small spring onion
 salt and coarsely ground pepper

Grate the orange rind. Cut the orange flesh free of pith and inside skin, then cut it into small pieces. Core the pears and cut them into small cubes. Toss them at once with the orange rind and flesh, lemon rind and juice and the honey. Cover and chill for 1–2 hours (overnight if the pears are hard).

   Shortly before you wish to serve the salad, grate the carrots coarsely. Finely chop both green and white parts of the spring onion, and mix with the carrots. Season well with salt and coarsely ground black pepper. Toss the pear mixture and its juice with the carrots. Taste, and adapt the seasoning if you wish.

PINK CELERIAC SALAD

For 4 first-course or side-dish helpings, use:

   1 cooked beetroot, about 6 oz (150 g)
   14 oz (350 g) celeriac
   6 tablespoons (6 × 15 ml spoons) cider vinegar
   2 tablespoons (2 × 15 ml spoons) water
   4 thin sticks celery
   10–12 cocktail gherkins
   2 dessertspoons (2 × 10 ml spoons) capers
   salt and pepper
   salad oil (not olive oil)

Peel the beetroot, and chop it into small pieces. Peel the celeriac and grate it coarsely. Put the beetroot and celeriac in separate bowls, and pour over each 3 tablespoons (3 × 15 ml spoons) of vinegar and 1 tablespoon (1 × 15 ml spoon) of water. Slice the celery thinly, chop the cocktail gherkins into small pieces (not finely) and mix them into the celeriac with the capers. Season both the beetroot and the celeriac mixture with salt and pepper and leave for 4–5 hours.

Just before serving, mix the beetroot and its crimson vinegar with the celeriac mixture. Add more salt and pepper if you wish. Pile the salad in a serving bowl, and trickle a little oil over it.

COMPOTE SALADS

Fresh or dried fruits, steeped or stewed (page 27), make excellent salads, especially when mixed with chopped fresh herbs or spices. Add cold, cooked or raw salad vegetables as well. Try, for instance, orange segments steeped in white wine, then drained and mixed with cucumber cubes and chopped fresh mint; it is delicious with cold lamb.

Spiced fruits are particularly good with strongly flavoured meats. A compote of cinnamon-flavoured plums or cherries goes well with duck, pigeon or hare. Drain it well, then serve it on the diners' plates like a relish, or in a separate small bowl.

Cinnamon-spiced, poached peaches or apricots make another good compote to serve as a salad. Drain and slice the fruit while still hot, then mix it with thinly sliced sweet green pepper, and pour a little of the poaching liquid back over both. Cool completely, then serve with curries, or with a hot staple-grain dish such as Polenta (page 22).

Other good sweet-sour cold salads can be made by mixing: blanched cauliflower sprigs with black grapes steeped in wine; cooked cubed potato with apple cubes steeped in cider; cooked, sliced green beans with cubed cooking pears poached in lemon-flavoured water; chopped peppers with grapefruit segments steeped in (diluted) sherry. Serve any of these with cold chicken, turkey or white fish, or with a vegetable curry or risotto.

Before you use a compote as a salad, let the fruit lie in its steeping or poaching liquid for 2–3 hours, so that it absorbs the liquid's flavour, softens (if hard) and cools (if cooked). Then, as a rule, drain it carefully before mixing it with salad ingredients or herbs. Add only dry flavourings; no oil and vinegar or creamy salad dressing is needed.

FENNEL AND YOGHURT SALAD

For 4–6 first-course or side-dish helpings, use:

> 1 cucumber, about 6–7 oz (150–175 g)
> salt
> 12–14 oz (300–350 g) fennel bulb
> ½ sweet red pepper
> 2 spring onions, green and white parts
> 1 good tablespoon (1 × 15 ml spoon) chopped parsley
> grated rind of 1 lemon
> a few drops of lemon juice
> a few drops of olive oil
> pepper
> ¼ pint (125 ml) natural yoghurt

Slice the cucumber thickly, then cut the slices into quarters. Salt them well, and leave on a tilted plate for 15 minutes. Slice the fennel thickly. Blanch it in salted boiling water for 2 minutes. Drain it and let it cool.

Finely chop the flesh of the pepper. Put a few bits aside. Chop both green and white parts of the spring onions. Cut the cooled fennel into small strips.

Mix the pepper, onions and fennel in a bowl, adding most of the parsley. Drain and mix in the cucumber. Sprinkle with the lemon rind, and a few drops of juice and oil. Grind a little pepper over the salad.

Pile the salad on a platter, and coat it with the yoghurt. Sprinkle the reserved scarlet pepper and green parsley on top.

KOHLRABI SALAD

This must be one of the simplest salads on record, but it is fresh-tasting and delicious.

For 4 first-course or side-dish helpings, use:

> 2–3 kohlrabi bulbs (see recipe)
> 2 teaspoons (2 × 5 ml spoons) salt
> 4 teaspoons (4 × 5 ml spoons) lemon juice
> 2–3 tablespoons (2–3 × 15 ml spoons) finely chopped fresh
>   thyme, marjoram or parsley or a mixture
> olive or walnut oil if you wish
> lemon wedges

You will need about 1 lb (450 g) of the vegetable after topping and tailing it. Do this, then grate the kohlrabi coarsely into quite thick shreds. Mix them at once with the salt and lemon juice and leave in a cool place for at least two hours.

Just before you serve the salad, mix in most of the herbs. Pile the salad in a bowl. Trickle a little oil over it if you wish. Sprinkle it with the rest of the herbs, and serve with lemon wedges to squeeze over each helping.

CRACKED WHEAT AND MELON SALAD

This salad is easy to make now that burghul (cracked wheat) is fairly widely available in our delicatessen and health-food shops.

For 6 first-course or side-dish helpings, use:

>   8 oz (200 g) burghul (cracked wheat)
>   ½ small melon
>   4 spring onions, green and white parts
>   3 tablespoons (3 × 15 ml spoons) chopped parsley
>   3 tablespoons (3 × 15 ml spoons) finely chopped fresh mint
>   (see note)
>   8 tablespoons (8 × 15 ml spoons) Apple Juice Salad Dressing
>   (page 93)

Soak the burghul in a lot of cold water for 30 minutes; it will swell up, so soak it in a large bowl. Drain, and squeeze out as much moisture as you can.

Take any seeds out of the melon and cube the flesh. Chop both the green and white parts of the spring onions. Mix the melon, onions, parsley and mint in a bowl. Add the burghul, and toss them all together. Trickle over the salad just enough dressing to make it moist but not soggy. (If you do not use all the dressing, keep the rest in the refrigerator to use as a standard dressing for other salads.)

Note: Do not try to make this salad with dried herbs; it is dull.

POLISH GREEN BEAN SALAD

This salad can consist simply of young French beans sliced diagonally, mixed with very thinly sliced rings of a small onion. They are simmered briefly in salted water containing a little lemon juice. When barely tender, they are drained, and sprinkled while still warm with a little finely chopped chervil and French dressing (page 92).

In a more elaborate version, the beans are mixed with very small cauliflower spriglets cooked like the beans but for a few moments longer. Both are then seasoned lightly with French dressing while still warm. When cooled, they are sprinkled with a mixture of sieved hard-boiled egg yolk and fine fried bread-crumbs (1 yolk to 2 tablespoons/2 × 15 ml spoons crumbs) and are bordered by the chopped egg whites.

In one luxurious version, the bean and cauliflower salad is sprinkled with finely crumbled cooked bacon, and is crowned with, or ringed by, whole hard-boiled egg yolks sprinkled with salad oil and paprika. The dominant gold and green look regal, provided the yolks have no trace of grey on them.

JELLIED BEETROOT SALAD

For 6 first-course or side-dish helpings, use:

1½ lb (750 g) young beetroot, boiled (see recipe)
2 tablespoons (2 × 15 ml spoons) lemon juice
8 fl oz (200 ml) cold water
3 teaspoons (3 × 5 ml spoons) gelatine
¼ pint (125 ml) orange juice
2 teaspoons (2 × 5 ml spoons) cider vinegar
1 dessertspoon (1 × 10 ml spoon) grated horseradish (bought)
1 dessertspoon (1 × 10 ml spoon) freshly grated orange rind
1 teaspoon (1 × 5 ml spoon) grated onion
1 teaspoon (1 × 5 ml spoon) table salt
4 oz (100 g) finely chopped young celery
crisp young lettuce leaves

If possible, use small, young raw beetroot, and boil them only until just tender. If you have to buy boiled beetroot, choose small firm ones with unbroken skins.

Cool home-boiled beetroot, then peel and dice them. Put them in a bowl and sprinkle with the lemon juice.

Pour the water into a large heatproof bowl, and scatter on the gelatine. When it softens, stand the bowl in very hot water, and stir until the gelatine dissolves. Remove from the heat, and stir in all the other ingredients except the beetroot, celery and lettuce leaves. Chill until just beginning to thicken. Fold in the beetroot with their juice, and the celery. Turn into a wetted 2-pint (1 litre) plain jelly mould or bowl, and chill until set. Make a 'bed' of the lettuce leaves and unmould the salad on to it.

CHINESE SALAD

For 4–6 first-course or side-dish helpings, use:

6 oz (150 g) bean sprouts
2 hard-boiled eggs
½ sweet red pepper
1 clove garlic
salt
Ginger Salad Dressing (page 94), using oil
½ medium cooked turnip, about 2 oz (50 g)
1 stick celery
3 cocktail gherkins
1 tablespoon (1 × 15 ml spoon) chopped parsley

Pour boiling water over the bean sprouts, drain them and leave them to cool under soft paper.

Chop the eggs and the flesh of the pepper into small pieces (not finely). Mix them together. Squeeze the garlic over them with a little salt. Then pour most of the dressing over the mixture.

Chop the turnip and thinly slice the celery and gherkins. Mix all three with the bean sprouts, using a fork. Then combine the mixture lightly with the dressed egg salad. Add the rest of the dressing if needed. Sprinkle with the chopped parsley.

SALADE MAISON

For 4–5 first-course or side-dish helpings, use:

4 sharp dessert apples, red-skinned if possible
1 dessertspoon (1 × 10 ml spoon) lemon or orange juice
2 sticks celery
1½ oz (35 g) walnut pieces
salt and pepper
3 teaspoons (3 × 5 ml spoons) grated orange rind
3 fl oz (75 ml) mayonnaise
4 medium tomatoes
flat lettuce leaves

Core the apples, chop them and toss them at once with the fruit juice. Slice the celery thinly, and chop the nuts into small fragments.

Drain the apples, keeping the juice. Mix the drained apples, celery and 1 oz (25 g) of the nuts; add a little seasoning and 1 teaspoon (1 × 5 ml spoon) of orange rind.

Pound or crush the rest of the nuts finely. Stir them into the mayonnaise with the reserved fruit juice and a second teaspoon (1 × 5 ml spoon) of orange rind. Season the mayonnaise, if you wish. Spoon it over the apple and celery salad.

Take out the tomato seeds, and chop the flesh.

Lay the lettuce leaves on a flat platter. Pile the apple and celery mixture on top. Arrange the chopped tomato in a scarlet ring round the piled salad. Scatter the remaining orange rind on the salad.

Note: If you use lemon juice, you may want to add a few drops of clear honey to the mayonnaise when you taste for seasoning.

SAUERKRAUT SALAD

For 4 first-course or side-dish helpings, use:

   1 lb (450 g) canned or bottled sauerkraut
   6 oz (150 g) black grapes
   ½ small sharp eating apple
   5 tablespoons (5 × 15 ml spoons) dry white wine
   2 teaspoons (2 × 5 ml spoons) clear honey
   salt and pepper

Rinse the sauerkraut under a cold running tap. Drain it thoroughly. Halve the grapes and pip them. Core and chop the apple, and toss it at once in 1 tablespoon (1 × 15 ml spoon) of the wine. Make a dressing by mixing the remaining wine and the honey. Combine the sauerkraut, grapes and apple, and toss them lightly in the dressing. Season with salt and pepper, pile in a serving bowl, and chill before serving.

FRUIT SLAW

We are sure you can make a standard cole slaw, so we are giving you a slightly unusual one instead.

For 4 first-course or side-dish helpings, use:

2 oz (50 g) dried apricots
1 lb (450 g) firm white cabbage
salt and pepper
2 slices fresh pineapple or 2 canned pineapple rings and a few drops of lemon juice
3 spring onions, green and white parts
2 tablespoons (2 × 15 ml spoons) chopped nuts (any kind except peanuts)
¼ pint (125 ml) Roquefort Salad Dressing (page 93) or as needed

Soak the dried apricots in warm water until tender but not yet soft. Drain and chop them. Shred the cabbage, discarding stalk and ribs. Season it well, and put it in a bowl with the apricots.

Chop the pineapple into very small pieces; do this over the cabbage so that the juice is not lost. Add the pineapple pieces to the cabbage. Include a few drops of lemon juice if using canned pineapple.

Chop both green and white parts of the spring onions. Crush the nuts almost (but not quite) to powder; they should still be grainy. Mix the spring onions and nuts into the salad. Taste, and add any extra seasoning needed.

Mix just enough dressing into the slaw to moisten it well. Very finely shredded cabbage may not need quite the full ¼ pint (125 ml). Serve the salad slightly chilled.

Note: If fresh pineapple juice is tart, add ¼–½ teaspoon (½–1 × 2.5 ml spoon) clear honey with the dressing.

PRESIDENT'S SLAW

For 4–6 first-course or side-dish helpings, use:

5 tablespoons (5 × 15 ml spoons) apple juice
2 oz (50 g) prunes
1 oz (25 g) seedless raisins
½ medium red cabbage, about 12 oz (300 g)
½ medium onion, about 2 oz (50 g)

1 green-skinned sharp dessert apple, about 3 oz (75 g)
2 oz (50 g) walnut pieces
grated rind of 1 small orange

For the dressing
3 tablespoons (3 × 15 ml spoons) apple juice
4 tablespoons (4 × 15 ml spoons) salad oil (not olive oil)
salt and pepper

Pour 4 tablespoons (4 × 15 ml spoons) of the apple juice over the prunes and raisins, and add just enough hot water to cover them. Leave them to steep for 1–2 hours.

Finely shred the cabbage, discarding the core and ribs. Chop the onion and mix it with the cabbage. Core and chop the apple, and mix at once with the last tablespoon (1 × 15 ml spoon) of the apple juice. Set aside. Chop the walnuts, and mix with the orange rind.

Drain the dried fruit. Take out the prune stones, and chop the flesh. Mix both dried fruits into the cabbage. Season well. Drain and add the apple, and most of the walnut–orange rind mixture. Pile the salad in a serving bowl.

Mix the apple juice and oil for the dressing in a bottle with a firm stopper. Season well, stopper the bottle and shake the dressing vigorously. Trickle the dressing over the slaw, and sprinkle with the rest of the walnut–orange rind mixture.

PRINCE CONSORT'S PLUM PUDDING

Although it looks solid, this is a beautifully light pudding inside.
If there is any left over, it will be almost as light if re-steamed in a
covered container, or it can be sliced and fried.

For 8 helpings, use:

1 lb (450 g) prunes
1½ pints (850 ml) water
1 lemon
1 oz (25 g) Barbados or similar brown sugar
margarine for greasing
2 large eggs
4 oz (100 g) margarine
4 oz (100 g) light soft brown sugar
a pinch of table salt
4 oz (100 g) soft wholemeal breadcrumbs
1½ oz (35 g) semolina

For Prune Sauce
1 teaspoon (1 × 5 ml spoon) arrowroot
½ pint (250 ml) juice from soaking and cooking the prunes
1 dessertspoon (1 × 10 ml spoon) demerara sugar
1 tablespoon (1 × 15 ml spoon) brandy or more if you wish

Steep the prunes in the water overnight. Next day, grate the rind
of half the lemon and pare off the rest. Squeeze the juice. Simmer
the prunes with the water, pared lemon rind, juice and the
Barbados sugar until soft. Strain over a saucepan, and keep the
liquid for the Prune Sauce; make it up to ½ pint (250 ml) with
water if you need to.

Cut the prunes in half and take out the stones. Grease the
inside of a 2 pint (1.1 litre) pudding basin thickly. Press enough
prunes into the fat, cut side down, to line the basin completely.
Shred any prunes left over. Separate the eggs.

Now beat the 4 oz (100 g) fat and the soft brown sugar until creamy, and beat in the egg yolks with the salt. Mix in the grated lemon rind, breadcrumbs, semolina and any shredded prunes. Whisk the egg whites until they just hold firm peaks, and fold them into the mixture. Turn it gently into the basin, and cover it tightly with greased foil. Steam the pudding for 2½–3 hours.

Just before it is ready, make the prune sauce. Mix the arrowroot to a smooth paste with a little of the prune juice. Warm the rest of the juice until very hot, then pour it on to the blended mixture, stirring all the time. Return the mixture to the saucepan, and bring it slowly to the boil, stirring without ceasing. Simmer gently for a few moments only. Stir in the sugar and let it dissolve, then add the brandy. Taste and add extra brandy if you wish.

Turn the pudding out on to a warmed serving plate. Offer the hot sauce separately, together with plenty of chilled whipped cream.

BERBAGE PUDDING

The old recipes for this traditional pudding use equal quantities of breadcrumbs and fat, and a little more jam; but we find the pudding too rich, and prefer the proportions below. It is a beautifully light pudding, more delicate than its rich, dark brown appearance suggests.

For 6–8 helpings, use:

>   lard for greasing
>   6 oz (150 g) wholemeal, wholewheat or high-bran bread-
>   crumbs
>   4 oz (100 g) shredded suet
>   4 oz (100 g) dark soft brown sugar
>   a pinch of table salt
>   3 tablespoons (3 × 15 ml spoons) smooth (not whole fruit)
>   strawberry or raspberry jam (see note)
>   1 egg
>   1 teaspoon (1 × 5 ml spoon) bicarbonate of soda
>   extra strawberry or raspberry jam for sauce

Grease a 1¾-pint (1 litre) pudding basin, and put a large pan of water on to boil. Mix together thoroughly all the ingredients except the egg, bicarbonate of soda and extra jam. Mix the soda with the egg, and blend it into the mixture. Turn the mixture into the basin, filling it only three-quarters full. Cover the basin tightly with foil, and steam for at least 3 hours. Just before the pudding is ready, warm enough extra jam to serve as a sauce. When it is ready, let the pudding stand in the basin at room temperature for a few moments to firm up, then turn it out and serve it with the sauce and with whipped cream.

Note: Strawberry jam is traditional, but we think sieved raspberry jam makes a better pudding.

POKEROUNCE

This old dish goes back to the Norman conquest. It is even older than the better known 'Poor Knights' and is also easier to make, as long as you do not mind sticky fingers.

For 4 helpings, use:

> 4 large slices wholemeal bread, $\frac{1}{2}$ inch (1 cm) thick, from a tin loaf
> 8 oz (200 g) honey
> a pinch of ground ginger
> a pinch of ground cinnamon
> a tiny pinch of ground black pepper
> about 64 pine-nut kernels, about $\frac{1}{2}$ oz (15 g)

Cut the crusts off the bread and toast it very lightly on both sides. Cut each slice into 4 small squares or rectangles. Put them in one layer on a well-warmed platter and keep them warm. Put the honey and spices, including the pepper, into a small saucepan, and melt the honey over very gentle heat. Simmer for not more than 2 minutes. Do not let the mixture boil or darken, or it will 'toffee'. Let it cool very slightly, then pour it over the toast. Stick 4 pine nuts upright in each piece of toast, like small stakes. Serve quickly while still hot.

The toasts look even more dramatic if left as 4 large slices with 16 nuts upright in each, but they are messier to make.

SPICED CIDER CURD PIE

Cheesecake is nourishing and popular in a lunch-box. You can make this one as either a double-crust pie, which is easy to pack, or as an open pie with a crumbly topping for use at home. For the double-crust pie, you will need about 8 oz (200 g) pastry, and for

an open pie about 5 oz (125 g) pastry and 2 tablespoons
(2 × 15 ml spoons) Sweet Crumble Topping (page 128).

For one 6½-inch (16 cm) sweet cheese pie, use:

margarine for greasing
wholemeal shortcrust pastry (page 124) as above
2 tablespoons (2 × 15 ml spoons) demerara sugar for sprink-
    ling or Sweet Crumble Topping (page 128)
10 oz (250 g) well-drained cottage cheese
4 tablespoons (4 × 15 ml spoons) double cream
6 oz (150 g) demerara sugar
1 teaspoon (1 × 5 ml spoon) ground ginger
¼ teaspoon (½ × 2.5 ml spoon) ground cinnamon
3 oz (75 g) pine-nut kernels, almonds or unsalted peanuts
2 dessertspoons (2 × 10 ml spoons) full-flavoured cider
2 egg whites

Grease a 6½-inch (16 cm) sandwich tin about 1½ inches (3–4 cm)
deep, with a removable bottom. Roll out the pastry and line the
tin. Let the top edge stand up slightly above the rim of the tin if
making a double-crust pie.

Sieve the cheese and mix it with the cream, sugar and spices.
Chop the nuts finely and mix them in. Stir in the cider. Beat the
egg whites until frothy, and stir them in. Turn the mixture into
the pie shell.

If making a double crust pie, cut out a piece of pastry to fit the
top of the tin. Damp the edge of the pastry shell, fit on the lid and
pinch the edges together to seal the pie. Brush the lid lightly with
water and sprinkle it with the 2 tablespoons (2 × 15 ml spoons)
demerara sugar. To complete an open pie, scatter the crumble
topping evenly over the cheesecake mixture.

Bake the cheesecake at 350° (130°C) Gas 4 for 1 hour.

ORANGE AND OAT CHEESECAKE

For 4 helpings, use:

For the rolled oat base
2 oz (50 g) margarine
3 oz (75 g) rolled oats
1 oz (25 g) muscovado sugar
½ teaspoon (1 × 2.5 ml spoon) ground cinnamon

For the cheesecake
2 oranges
extra orange juice if necessary
¼ oz (8 g) (½ pkt) gelatine
8 oz (200 g) sieved cottage cheese
2 oz (50 g) light muscovado sugar
lemon juice if you wish
grated rind of 1 lemon

Grate the rinds off both oranges, and squeeze the juice. Make it up to ¼ pint (125 ml) with extra juice if you need to. Put the orange juice in a saucepan and scatter on the gelatine. When it softens, heat the juice gently until fairly warm, take off the heat and stir until the gelatine dissolves. Leave to cool.

Grease a 6-inch (15 cm) cake tin with a removable base, with ¼ oz (8 g) of the fat. Melt the remaining fat, stir in the oats, sugar and cinnamon, and mix well. Press the mixture firmly into the bottom of the tin in an even layer. Chill until firm.

Beat the cheese, light muscovado sugar and half the orange rind together lightly until well blended. (Keep the rest of the rind for topping the cheesecake.)

When the orange-juice jelly is thickening and almost at setting point, mix it lightly, a few spoonfuls at a time, into the cheese mixture. Taste, and squeeze in a little fresh lemon juice if you wish; it usually improves it. Turn the mixture quickly into the cake tin, and leave to set.

When the cheescake is fully set and firm, unmould it. Sprinkle the top with the remaining orange rind and the grated rind of a lemon. This simple topping both looks good and gives a refreshing tang to the dessert.

WHOLEMEAL AND WALNUT ICE CREAM

For 4 helpings, use:

    ¾ pint (425 ml) double cream
    3 oz (75 g) demerara sugar
    2–3 teaspoons (2–3 × 5 ml spoons) rum
    2 oz (50 g) stale wholemeal bread without crusts
    1 oz (25 g) coarsely ground walnuts

Turn the refrigerator to its coldest setting well before making the ice cream. Whip the cream until it just holds soft peaks, gradually adding 1 oz (25 g) of the sugar, and the rum. Divide the cream between two freezer containers, leaving plenty of room in each. Cover, and freeze in the ice-making compartment of the refrigerator for about 1 hour.

Crumble the bread coarsely, mix with the rest of the sugar, and put in a very low oven until crisped. Cool the crumbs, and mix them with the nuts. Fold the crumb mixture into the half-frozen cream with a fork. Cover, and put back in the ice-making compartment until frozen all through (but not rock-hard).

CHESTNUT CREAM FLAN

For 6–8 helpings, use:

For the flan case
3½ oz (85 g) butter or margarine
6 oz (150 g) breakfast cereal bran flakes
3 tablespoons (3 × 15 ml spoons) clear honey

For the filling
¼ pint (125 ml) double or whipping cream
9 oz (225 g) unsweetened chestnut purée
2 tablespoons (2 × 15 ml spoons) clear honey
1 tablespoon (1 × 15 ml spoon) rum

For the topping
½ oz (15 g) butter or margarine
1 tablespoon (1 × 15 ml spoon) clear honey
1 oz (25 g) breakfast cereal bran flakes

Make the flan case first. Use ½ oz (15 g) of the fat to grease an 8½–9 inch (22 cm) flan ring on a baking sheet. Crush the bran flakes coarsely. Melt the remaining fat and honey together, and stir in the flakes. Mix well. Press the mixture firmly into the sides and over the base of the flan ring and baking sheet. Bake at 350°F (180°C) Gas 4 for 10 minutes. Cool slightly, remove the ring and leave the case to cool completely.

Whip the cream for the filling until stiff. Beat the chestnut purée until soft and smooth, beating in the honey and rum. Beat the cream into the chestnut mixture. Fill the cream evenly into the cooled case.

Make the topping. Melt the fat and honey together in a small saucepan. Stir in the flakes with a fork, then spread them on a metal plate or baking sheet to cool. Sprinkle them over the flan.

Note: You can use this topping to decorate 4 individual ice creams or to cover the top of a 6–7 inch (15–17 cm) cake over a jam glaze coating.

CARROT AND ALMOND CAKE

Offer this beautifully moist, light cake with cream as a dessert or use it at tea-time.

For one 7-inch (17.5 cm) cake, use:

> margarine for greasing
> 10 oz (250 g) carrots
> 5 eggs
> 7 oz (175 g) light muscovado sugar
> $\frac{1}{2}$ lemon
> 8 oz (200 g) ground almonds
> 2 tablespoons (2 × 15 ml spoons) wholemeal flour
> 2 tablespoons (2 × 15 ml spoons) white flour
> 1 teaspoon (1 × 5 ml spoon) ground cinnamon
> a pinch of ground cloves

Grease a deep 7-inch (17.5 cm) cake tin.

Grate the carrots; allowing for wastage, you should have 8 oz (200 g) grated carrot. Separate the eggs. Beat the yolks until frothy. Add the sugar, and beat together until pale, smooth and creamy. Grate the rind of the $\frac{1}{2}$ lemon, and squeeze its juice. Lightly mix them into the egg and sugar mixture.

Mix $\frac{1}{3}$ of the carrots into the egg and sugar mixture, then $\frac{1}{3}$ of the almonds. Repeat the process twice, using up all the carrots and almonds. Mix together the wholemeal and white flours and the spices, and stir them in. Beat the egg whites until stiff and glossy. Stir 4 tablespoons (4 × 15 ml spoons) into the mixture, then fold in the rest.

Turn the mixture gently into the prepared tin. Bake it at 350°F (180°C) Gas 4 for 1 hour. Cover it loosely with paper if it is already brown, lower the heat to 325°F (160°C) Gas 3, and bake for another 15–20 minutes or until the cake has loosened slightly from the sides of the tin. Turn it out and cool on a wire rack.

If you like, you can coat the top of the cooled cake with Jam Glaze (page 130), then with Toasted Nut Brittle Topping (page 129).

CAROB LAYER CAKE

If you have never tried using carob powder, take this chance. It comes from a plant with the delightful name of St John's bread, and is a sweet powder which tastes almost like chocolate. Although the powder is finer than cocoa, you can use it in the same way in cakes.

For one 7½-inch (18 cm) layer cake, use:

    margarine for greasing
    flour for dusting
    1 tablespoon (1 × 15 ml spoon) margarine
    8 fl oz (200 ml) natural yoghurt
    1 teaspoon (1 × 5 ml spoon) vanilla essence
    4 oz (100 g) 81% extraction flour
    4 oz (100 g) wholemeal flour
    2 oz (50 g) carob powder
    2½ oz (65 g) nibbed almonds
    4 fl oz (100 ml) hot strong black coffee
    1 teaspoon (1 × 5 ml spoon) bicarbonate of soda
    Honey Icing (page 131)

Grease and flour lightly two 7½-inch (18 cm) sandwich cake tins. Heat the oven to 350°F (180°C) Gas 4.

Soften the margarine in a mixing bowl. Warm the honey and add it with the yoghurt; beat thoroughly until all three ingredients are fully blended. Add the vanilla essence while beating.

Sieve on to a sheet of paper both flours and the carob powder. Add them to the liquid mixture in two or three parts, beating well each time. Include any bran left in the sieve, and the almonds.

Put the hot coffee in a fair-sized bowl or jug, and stir in the soda; it will bubble up. Tip it at once into the cake mixture, and stir in quickly. Still working quickly, turn the mixture into the two tins, and smooth and level the tops. Bake for about 25 minutes until the cakes shrink slightly from the sides of the tins. Cool in the tins for 5 minutes. Turn out very gently (the cakes are fragile), and finish cooling on a wire rack. When cold, cover one cake evenly with icing. Put the second cake layer on top and ice it, swirling the icing with a knife.

Serve as a dessert, with whipped cream.

BAKING NATURALLY

Breads and Rolls

WHOLEMEAL BREAD AND ROLLS (Basic recipe)
For two 13-oz (350 g) tin or bun loaves and 10–12 rolls, use:

    1–1½ pints (500–850 ml) warm water (see recipe)
    2¼ lb (1 kg) wholemeal flour (strong flour if possible)
    ½ oz (15 g) table salt
    2 oz (50 g) margarine or lard
    1 oz (25 g) fresh yeast or ½ oz (15 g) dried yeast and 1
      level teaspoon (1 × 5 ml spoon) clear honey
    oil for greasing
    extra margarine or lard for greasing

Vary the quantity of water you use to suit the flour. The milling, the flour's quality, even the weather, may make it need more or less water than usual. If you bake the bread in tins, make the dough slightly wetter than for bun loaves or rolls.

Mix the flour and salt in a large bowl. Make a hollow in the centre. Melt the fat, and leave it in the pan to cool while you cream the yeast with a little of the water, and add the honey if dried yeast is used. Put the yeast, fat and 1 pint (500 ml) of the water into the hollow, and mix it in by hand until you have a fairly solid dough. Add more water if the dough still seems dry or if you are going to bake all the bread in tins (you can make 4 loaves instead of rolls if you wish).

Knead the dough hard by hand, like a punch-bag, using the heels of your hands and your knuckles. Work it for 10–15 minutes until it becomes smooth and elastic.

Put the bowl in a large, lightly oiled polythene bag. Then either put it in the refrigerator for about 12 hours before raising it, or in a warm place for about 2 hours until doubled in bulk. A good place to raise it in modern days is on a (barely warm) radiator or electric plate-warming unit. With time to spare, you can simply leave it in a modern, centrally heated or reasonably warm kitchen overnight. This is probably best because the more slowly the dough rises the better.

When the dough is raised, form it into a more or less square shape on a lightly floured surface. Cut it into 4 equal portions. Grease two 7½ × 3¾ × 2 inch (19 × 9 × 5 cm) loaf tins (if baking 2 tin loaves) and a baking sheet (for bun loaves or rolls). Put one portion of dough into each tin, if you use them; fill the tins only half-full, and press the dough well down into the corners. Shape bun loaves into rounds and cut a deep cross in the top of each—not only to make a conventional, attractive shape but to let air and heat penetrate the dough quickly.

Rolls can be any shape you like, but a useful one is to make a flattish round like a hamburger and then fold it in half into a 'fanlight' shape. This is the traditional Parker House Roll shape. It is a convenient one because you can put any 'extra' such as chopped herbs, a little grated cheese or a few sultanas on the round before folding it, and it will be baked in.

Leave the loaves and rolls in a warm place for 45 minutes–1 hour. Rolls will have risen sooner but you can leave them with the bread unless it is more convenient to cook them separately first. As soon as the dough is swollen and yielding, you can bake it. Bake both loaves and rolls at 425°F (220°C) Gas 7 for 20 minutes. Then take out any rolls, and bake loaves for another 10 minutes. Turn the heat down to 325°F (160°C) Gas 3 and bake for 15–20 minutes more. Turn the bread on to a wire rack to cool—and enjoy it.

CROWN RYE BREAD

Take care when making—and eating—rye bread. Don't try to 'beat the clock' in either process. Rye bread is slower to raise and bake than wheat breads. (Some people say you can only make it successfully with sour dough, although we think this recipe proves otherwise.) As for eating it, don't be over-enthusiastic at first. It can 'lie heavy' as our medieval ancestors knew (and complained about). A little goes a long way; and a lot, eaten when you are not yet used to it, can make you really uncomfortable with that inelegant complaint, wind.

Baked with patience and eaten in small amounts to begin with, rye bread can be a nutty, new tasting experience. These loaves are unusually light, with no sour flavour. They are particularly good, as the creator of the recipe, Patricia Jacobs, recommends, cut thin, spread with full-fat soft cheese and broken walnuts, and made into sandwiches. Patricia Jacobs gave us the recipe from her excellent baking book, *The Best Bread Book* (Harwood-Smart, 1975).

For four 6-inch (15 cm) loaves, use:

> 1 oz (25 g) fresh yeast or ½ oz (15 g) dried yeast and 1 teaspoon (1 × 5 ml spoon) molasses
> ½ pint (250 ml) warm water
> 2 lb (900 g) strong white flour
> 1 lb (450 g) rye flour
> 1 pint (500 ml) skim milk from dry milk powder and water
> 4 tablespoons (4 × 15 ml spoons) molasses
> 4 teaspoons (4 × 5 ml spoons) salt
> 4 tablespoons (4 × 15 ml spoons) sunflower oil
> fat for greasing
> extra warm water as needed
> crushed wheat as needed

Cream the yeast with a little of the ½ pint (250 ml) warm water, and the teaspoon (5 ml spoon) molasses if using dried yeast, and leave until bubbling. Blend with the rest of the water to dissolve it. Sift the white flour into a large mixing bowl. Mix in the rye flour, then the yeast liquid, skim milk, molasses, salt and oil. Knead in the bowl to make a pliable dough. Put the bowl into a greased polythene bag and leave the dough to rise for at least 2 hours. When well raised, form it into 4 round loaves. Put them on a lightly greased baking sheet. Cut a fairly deep cross in the top of each loaf. (After baking, they will have opened out, making the loaves crown-shaped.) Put the loaves on the sheet back in the bag, and leave to prove for at least 30 minutes. Sprinkle with warm water and crushed wheat. Bake at 375°F (190°C) Gas 5 for about 40 minutes, until the loaves sound hollow on the bottom when tapped. Cool on a wire rack. For sandwiches, wrap in foil when cooled, store for a day in an airtight tin, then cut thinly.

AMERICAN CORNBREAD

For two 11-oz (275 g) loaves, use:

> 1 tablespoon (1 × 15 ml spoon) butter
> 2 eggs
> ½ pint (250 ml) milk
> 2 tablespoons (2 × 15 ml spoons) granulated sugar
> 4 oz (100 g) plain white flour

8 oz (200 g) corn meal (polenta, maize meal)
1 teaspoon (1 × 5 ml spoon) salt
3 teaspoons (3 × 5 ml spoons) baking powder
melted butter for brushing

Melt the butter without letting it get hot; take it off the heat. Beat the eggs into the milk with the sugar, and add them to the butter. Mix the flour, corn meal, salt and baking powder in a bowl; make a hollow in the centre, and pour in the liquid. Blend quickly, as lightly as you can; do not over-mix.

Grease two 7½ × 3¾ × 2 inch (19 × 9 × 5 cm) loaf tins, and turn in the cornbread mixture. Brush the tops with a little melted butter. Bake at 400°F (200°C) Gas 6 for about 20 minutes, until slightly shrunk from the tins. Cool in the tins for 10 minutes, then finish cooling on a wire rack. Use like any other bread, for breakfast or with a main course. Cornbread is especially good with a grilled chicken dish or with ham. It also makes classic American stuffings for poultry.

Buns, Cakes and Biscuits

CLAPPERS

For 16–20 clappers, use:

6 oz (150 g) fine oatmeal
2 oz (50 g) 81% extraction flour
½ teaspoon (1 × 2.5 ml spoon) salt
¼ teaspoon (½ × 2.5 ml spoon) bicarbonate of soda
1 oz (25 g) bacon fat or lard or a piece of fat pork rind
3–5 fl oz (75–125 ml) hot water
oatmeal for dusting
fat for greasing

Mix together the oatmeal, flour, salt and bicarbonate of soda. Melt the fat and mix it in. Add enough almost-boiling water to make a fairly stiff dough. Turn it on to a board dusted well with fine oatmeal, and knead for 2–3 minutes. Roll it out thinly, and cut into 3¼-inch (8 cm) rounds. Thinly grease a griddle or heavy frying pan, put it over moderate heat, and 'bake' the oatcakes, a few at a time, until they are patchily brown underneath. Flip them over with a palette knife, and bake the second sides. Do not add extra fat if you can help it; the oatcakes should not fry.

For labour-free although slightly less tasty oatcakes, bake them on ungreased baking sheets in the oven at 350°F (180°C) Gas 4, for 20 minutes. They should be evenly browned and crisp.

BUCKWHEAT BUNS OR 'MUFFINS'

For 10 buns or 'muffins', use:

> margarine for greasing
> 1 small onion
> 2 tablespoons (2 × 15 ml spoons) margarine
> 1 tablespoon (1 × 15 ml spoon) flaked peanuts
> 8 oz (200 g) buckwheat flour
> 3 tablespoons (3 × 15 ml spoons) wholemeal flour
> 1 teaspoon (1 × 5 ml spoon) baking powder
> ½ teaspoon (1 × 2.5 ml spoon) bicarbonate of soda
> ¼ teaspoon (½ × 2.5 ml spoon) salt
> 3 teaspoons (3 × 5 ml spoons) soy sauce
> 2 eggs
> 8 fl oz (200 ml) water

Grease ten 2½-inch (6 cm) deep bun tins. Chop the onion, and fry it gently in 1 tablespoon (1 × 15 ml spoon) of the fat until lightly browned. Toast the flaked peanuts under the grill until light brown, shaking the pan to brown them evenly. Shake together, in a mixing bowl, the two flours, baking powder and bicarbonate of soda, and rub in the second tablespoon (1 × 15 ml spoon) fat. Add the onion and its frying fat, the peanuts and salt. Mix the soy sauce and eggs into the water until well blended. Pour on to the dry ingredients, and mix to a soft dough or paste. Lightly turn the mixture into the bun tins, and bake at 375°F (190°C) Gas 5 for about 20 minutes. Cool on a wire rack, and eat like bread rolls with any savoury dish, or with butter and cheese.

BRAN SCONES

For 10–12 scones, use:

> 3 oz (75 g) wholemeal flour
> 4 oz (100 g) plain white flour
> 1 oz (25 g) natural wheat bran
> a small pinch of salt

1 teaspoon (1 × 5 ml spoon) bicarbonate of soda
1 teaspoon (1 × 5 ml spoon) cream of tartar
2 oz (50 g) margarine
1 oz (25 g) light soft brown sugar
1 egg
3 fl oz (75 ml) sour milk or as needed
2 oz (50 g) sultanas or seedless raisins
fat for greasing
milk for brushing scones

Shake together in a mixing bowl the two flours, bran, salt and
leavening. Rub in the margarine. Sieve and stir in the sugar. Beat
the egg with the milk, make a hollow in the dry ingredients, and
pour in the liquid. Mix to a soft dough as lightly as possible,
adding the fruit. Turn the dough on to a well-floured surface, and
pat out into a sheet about ¾ inch (2 cm) thick. Cut into rounds
with a 2½-inch (6 cm) cutter. Gather up the trimmings, press them
together, flatten and cut out more rounds. Put the scones on a
lightly greased baking sheet and brush the tops with a little milk.
Heat the oven to 425°F (220°C) Gas 7 and bake the scones for 10
minutes. Cool them on a wire rack. Use them, split and spread
with margarine (or curd or cottage cheese), for breakfast or for a
packed meal.

APRICOT BRANNOCKS

For 20–24 brannocks, use:

2 oz (50 g) dried apricots
6 oz (150 g) plain white flour
3 oz (75 g) wholemeal flour
1 oz (25 g) natural wheat bran
1 teaspoon (1 × 5 ml spoon) baking powder
½ teaspoon (1 × 2.5 ml spoon) salt
2 oz (50 g) Barbados or similar brown sugar
1 oz (25 g) margarine
2 tablespoons (2 × 15 ml spoons) clear honey
1 egg
1 teaspoon (1 × 5 ml spoon) bicarbonate of soda
4 fl oz (100 ml) milk
fat for greasing

Soak the apricots in cold water overnight. Drain, and reserve
4 fl oz (100 ml) of the soaking liquid. Squeeze apricots dry and

chop very finely. Shake together the flours, bran, baking powder and salt in a mixing bowl; mix in the sugar, being careful to break up any lumps. In a saucepan, melt the margarine and honey together without letting them get hot. Beat the egg until liquid. Dissolve the bicarbonate of soda in the milk.

Make a hollow in the centre of the dry goods, and pour in all the liquids, including the reserved soaking liquid. Stir only until just blended. The mixture should still be lumpy. Fork in, or lightly mix in, the dried apricots. Grease twenty-four 2½-inch (6 cm) bun tins, and turn in the mixture lightly, filling the tins only two-thirds full. Bake at 400°F (200°C) Gas 6 for about 20 minutes. Loosen from the tins with a palette knife. Serve hot for breakfast, or cold, split and filled with mild soft cheese and apricot jam for a packed meal or light lunch.

SWEET RYE AND BUTTERMILK 'BREAD'

More like a cake, this dark, spongy, steamed bread is excellent for supper 'afters' with creamy curd cheese or with stem ginger in syrup.

For one 2-lb (900 g) round loaf, use:

> margarine for greasing
> 6 oz (150 g) rye flour
> 6 oz (150 g) wholemeal flour
> 4 oz (100 g) fine oatmeal
> 1 dessertspoon (1 × 10 ml spoon) bicarbonate of soda
> 1 teaspoon (1 × 5 ml spoon) table salt
> ¼ pint (125 ml) molasses
> ¾ pint (375 ml) buttermilk

Grease a 2¾–3-pint (1.5–1.7 litres) cake tin or a charlotte mould about 6 inches (15 cm) across and 4 inches (10 cm) deep.

Shake together both flours, the oatmeal, soda and salt in a large bowl. Warm the molasses and buttermilk until just tepid. Stir them into the dry mixture lightly, until fully blended. The dough will be spongy. Turn the mixture gently into the prepared tin; it should have at least 1 inch (2.5 cm) headspace. Cover the tin securely with foil. Put it into a pan containing enough simmering water to come half-way up its sides. Let it simmer for 3 hours with the pan covered; top up the water once or twice if you need to.

When ready, lift out the tin and uncover the bread. Let it stand in the tin for 15 minutes, then ease it from the sides of the tin with a round-bladed knife and turn it gently on to a wire rack to cool. Let it stand for several hours before cutting it, or close-wrap and freeze it.

STEAMED SWEET CORNBREAD

Dark steamed Boston Brown Bread made with corn meal and dried fruit is given in many cookery books. This sweet golden bread made with whole kernel sweet corn is more unusual and versatile. Try it with a light savoury dish such as grilled bacon or with grilled pineapple rings as a supper dessert; or slice it to eat plain with mid-morning coffee or for tea.

For 2 small loaves or 16 slices, use:

   6 oz (150 g) plain white flour
   8 oz (200 g) yellow corn meal (polenta, maize meal)
   3 teaspoons (3 × 5 ml spoons) baking powder
   $\frac{1}{4}$ teaspoon ($\frac{1}{2}$ × 2.5 ml spoon) table salt
   4 oz (100 g) light muscovado sugar
   3 eggs
   3 tablespoons (3 × 15 ml spoons) vegetable oil
   $\frac{1}{2}$ pint (250 ml) milk or as needed
   1 × 11$\frac{1}{2}$ oz (1 × 326 g) can whole kernel sweet corn
   margarine for greasing

Shake all the dry ingredients together in a mixing bowl, and sieve in the sugar. In a smaller bowl, beat the eggs, oil and milk together. Drain the sweet corn well, and purée or mash it. Choose a pan (see note) which will hold 2 tins about 7$\frac{1}{2}$ × 3$\frac{3}{4}$ × 2 inches deep (19 × 9 × 5 cm) and put in enough hot water to come half-way up the sides of the tins. Grease the tins, and turn half the mixture into each. Cover tightly with foil. Put the tins in the pan, cover it and half-steam the loaves for 2 hours. Top up the water with extra boiling water if you need to. When ready, uncover the loaves and cool them in the tins, then turn them on to a wire rack for 1 hour to firm up. Wrap and store for 12 hours before cutting.

Note: An oval pot-roasting tin or a fish kettle is suitable as a steaming pan.

TRINIDAD LOAF CAKE (Coconut and peanut cake)

This light sweet loaf cake goes well with any banana dessert. It is also good plain, or spread with peanut butter and a sharp jam or jelly.

For two 1¼-lb (600 g) cakes, use:

    4 oz (100 g) seedless raisins
    4 oz (100 g) margarine
    6 oz (150 g) light muscovado sugar
    2 oz (50 g) flaked (unsalted) peanuts
    10 oz (250 g) desiccated coconut
    14 oz (400 g) wholemeal self-raising flour
    a pinch of table salt
    a pinch of ground cinnamon
    1 egg
    7 fl oz (175 ml) milk
    1 teaspoon (1 × 5 ml spoon) vanilla essence
    extra margarine for greasing
    desiccated coconut for sprinkling

Boil a little water in a saucepan, drop in the raisins, and leave to stand, off the heat, for 2–3 minutes. Drain the fruit and cool.

Cream the margarine and sugar. Add the nuts, raisins and all the dry ingredients. Beat the egg into the milk, and add the essence. Blend them thoroughly into the main mixture. Work with your hands for a moment or two to make a yielding dough. Grease two 7½ × 3¾ × 2 inch (19 × 9 × 5 cm) loaf tins. Turn in the mixture and press well down into the corners. Level and smooth the tops of the loaves. Sprinkle them with coconut. Bake at 375°F (190°C) Gas 5 for 35–40 minutes until the cakes are golden and firm, and slightly loose from the sides of the tins. Cool on a wire rack.

FRUIT GINGERBREAD

This moist gingerbread makes excellent supper 'afters' with a sweet sauce, or with mild cheese.

For one 11 × 7 inch (28 × 18 cm) slab, 6 squares or 20 fingers, use:

    3 cooked prunes
    2 oz (50 g) crystallized ginger

3 oz (75 g) molasses or treacle
5 oz (125 g) clear honey
6 oz (150 g) margarine
8 oz (200 g) 81% extraction flour
1 teaspoon (1 × 5 ml spoon) bicarbonate of soda
$\frac{1}{4}$ teaspoon ($\frac{1}{2}$ × 2.5 ml spoon) table salt
1 dessertspoon (1 × 10 ml spoon) ground ginger
1 dessertspoon (1 × 10 ml spoon) ground cinnamon
3 oz (75 g) Barbados or similar brown sugar
3 oz (75 g) seedless raisins
extra margarine for greasing

Finely chop the prunes and ginger together and set them aside.
Set the oven to heat to 350°F (180°C) Gas 4. While heating, warm the molasses or treacle tin in the oven, without a lid, to make measuring easier.

Melt together in a saucepan, the molasses, treacle, honey and margarine. Take the pan off the heat as soon as they melt. Mix the flour, bicarbonate of soda, salt, spices and sugar in a mixing bowl. Make a hollow in the centre, and pour in the melted mixture. Add the chopped prunes and ginger and the raisins. Stir thoroughly until blended. Lightly grease a shallow 11 × 7 inch (28 × 18 cm) baking tin. Turn in the mixture. Bake it for 20 minutes. Lower the heat to 325°F (160°C) Gas 3 and bake for 20–25 minutes more or until the gingerbread is firm in the centre. Cool in the tin. When cold, store in one slab in an airtight tin, ready to cut into squares or fingers when you want them.

DIGESTIVE BISCUITS

Like Clappers (page 116), digestive biscuits are good with cheese at any meal. They are also good on their own, with mid-morning coffee.

For 12 biscuits, use:

1 tablespoon (1 × 15 ml spoon) light soft brown sugar
3 oz (75 g) wholemeal flour
1 oz (25 g) plain white flour
1 oz (25 g) medium oatmeal
$\frac{1}{2}$ teaspoon (1 × 2.5 ml spoon) baking powder
a pinch of salt
2 oz (50 g) butter or margarine

2 tablespoons (2 × 15 ml spoons) milk
fine oatmeal for dusting
margarine for greasing

Crush or sieve the sugar if necessary. Mix it with the flours, oatmeal, baking powder and salt. Rub in the fat and bind to a pliable paste with the milk. Knead lightly on a floured board, then roll out to just under ¼ inch (5 mm) in thickness. Cut out rounds, using a 2½-inch (6 cm) cutter. Lay the biscuits on a lightly greased baking sheet, and prick each biscuit in three or four places with a fork. Bake at 350°F (180°C) Gas 4 for 15–20 minutes. Cool on the sheet, then store in an airtight tin. The biscuits keep excellently but can be re-crisped in the oven before serving if you wish.

CAROB AND WALNUT BISCUITS

For 24–30 biscuits, use:

3 oz (75 g) softened butter
2 fl oz (50 ml) clear honey
¼ teaspoon (½ × 2.5 ml spoon) salt
½ teaspoon (1 × 2.5 ml spoon) vanilla essence
2 tablespoons (2 × 15 ml spoons) sifted carob powder
1 egg
2 oz (50 g) self-raising wholemeal flour
2 oz (50 g) chopped walnuts

Use a very little of the butter to grease baking sheets. Beat together until fully blended all the ingredients except the flour and nuts. Fold these in. Drop rounded teaspoonfuls (5 ml spoonfuls) of the mixture on the baking sheets, well spaced apart. Bake at 350°F (180°C) Gas 4 for 12 minutes. Cool on the baking sheets.

Pastry

WHOLEMEAL SHORTCRUST PASTRY (Basic recipe)

For about 10 oz (250 g) prepared pastry, use:

> 6 oz (150 g) wholemeal flour
> a pinch of table salt
> 1 teaspoon (1 × 5 ml spoon) baking powder
> 1½ oz (35 g) margarine
> 1½ oz (35 g) lard or white vegetable fat
> cold water to mix

Shake together the flour, salt and baking powder in a bowl. Rub in the fats until the mixture is like fine crumbs. Mix in enough water to make a pliant dough which leaves the sides of the bowl clean. Leave in a cool place, covered, for 30 minutes. Roll out, and use as you wish.

RICH WHOLEMEAL SHORTCRUST PASTRY

For about 10 oz (250 g) prepared pastry, use:

> 2 oz (50 g) margarine
> 6 oz (150 g) wholemeal self-raising flour
> a pinch of salt
> 1 egg yolk
> 1 tablespoon (1 × 15 ml spoon) caster sugar
> about 1 fl oz (25 ml) cold water to mix

Rub the fat into the flour and salt until the mixture is crumbly. Beat the egg yolk with the sugar, and mix it into the dry ingredients with enough cold water to make a light but firm dough.

CRUMB PASTRY (Basic recipe)

For pastry to make one 8-inch (20 cm) flan case or tart shell, use:

> 8 oz (200 g) biscuits or similar crumbs (see recipe)
> 2–3 tablespoons (2–3 × 15 ml spoons) of any solid flavouring, e.g. grated cheese
> 3–4 oz (75–100 g) butter or margarine
> up to 2 oz (50 g) sweetening (for sweet pastry)
> other flavouring(s) to taste
> margarine for greasing

Make the crumbs. Break up biscuits or similar goods roughly. Place between two sheets of stout paper; the top sheet is needed to prevent the crumbs scattering. Roll a stout rolling pin over the crumbs, to crush them. Make fine even crumbs or the pastry may contain air-holes.

Mix the crumbs with any savoury or sweet solid flavouring you want to use. Melt the fat and any sweetening, in a well-warmed saucepan. As soon as they melt, take the pan off the heat and cool for 2–3 minutes (especially if using cheese). Then mix with the crumbs and any other flavourings. Press the mixture into an 8-inch (20 cm) greased flan ring on a baking sheet, or a pie plate. If lining both sides and bottom, line the sides first; they must not collapse. The bottom can be patched with different crumbs if too thin, or can rest on a plate.

Chill the shell for 20 minutes. Then use it as it is, or bake it at 325°F (160°C) Gas 3 for 10–15 minutes until firm and slightly crisp. Cool. Fill, and reheat or re-bake if you wish.

Note: Dry crumbs, e.g. crispbread crumbs, may need extra fat.

Alternative

PORRIDGE OAT PASTRY

For pastry to make one 8-inch (20 cm) flan case, use:

    4 oz (100 g) rolled oats
    4 oz (100 g) 81% extraction flour
    a pinch of salt
    4 oz (100 g) hard block margarine
    1 egg
    extra margarine for greasing

Shake together in a mixing bowl the oats, flour and salt. Rub in the margarine. Beat the egg until fluid, and mix in. Grease the inside of an 8-inch (20 cm) flan ring or loose-bottomed cake sandwich tin. Press the pastry evenly into the tin, to line it. Bake empty for 10–12 minutes at 375°F (190°C) Gas 5 or fill and bake at the same temperature for about 35 minutes or as needed to cook the filling.

WHOLEMEAL PUDDING CRUST PASTRY (Basic recipe)

Use this pastry just like suet crust pastry for meat or fruit puddings, roly-poly pudding or dumplings. This quantity will line
and cover a 2-pint (1.1. litre) pudding basin.

For 14 oz (400 g) prepared pastry, use:

> 3 oz (75 g) plain flour
> 4 oz (100 g) wholemeal flour
> 1 oz (25 g) wholemeal breadcrumbs
> ¼ teaspoon (½ × 2.5 ml spoon) salt
> 1 teaspoon (1 × 5 ml spoon) baking powder
> 3 oz (75 g) hard margarine
> about ¼ pint (125 ml) pint cold water

Mix together the flours, breadcrumbs, salt and baking powder.
Flake the fat, and mix it in. Add enough cold water to make a firm
dough. Knead lightly, then use as you wish.

DRESSING UP

Coatings and Toppings

COATINGS AND TOPPINGS TO USE

WHOLEMEAL BREADCRUMBS

1. *Soft breadcrumbs* for stuffings and other dishes are most easily made by putting fresh bread into the goblet of an electric blender with the motor running. Alternatively, slice the bread and dry it slightly, then grate it.
2. To make *dried crumbs*, dry bits of bread in a low oven, then crush them between two sheets of stout paper with a rolling pin. Make *browned crumbs* in the same way but leave them in the oven longer, until lightly coloured; use crusts or toast for making browned crumbs or 'raspings' too.
3. For *buttered crumbs*, melt 2 tablespoons (2 × 15 ml spoons) butter for each 4 oz (100 g) soft crumbs in a frying pan. Turn the crumbs over in the fat until well coated but barely coloured if at all. Cool them on soft kitchen paper, and store for up to a week in the refrigerator, loosely covered. Buttered crumbs brown more evenly than fried crumbs on dishes grilled or baked for more than a few minutes, and are less work to make. To make *fried crumbs*, turn the crumbs in the fat until evenly browned and crisp; use them on baked and other savoury dishes ready for serving. You can vary their flavour by mixing them with crumbled hard-boiled egg yolk or bacon, or with grated cheese.

OTHER COATINGS AND TOPPINGS

1. Make plain or sweet *biscuit crumbs* as described under Crumb Pastry on page 125. Use them in the same ways as breadcrumbs; also for coating cakes, lining a soufflé dish, and sprinkling over ice cream and creamy desserts. Use stale, dried or lightly fried plain *cake crumbs*, parkin or crushed macaroon crumbs in the same ways. (Do not store these fried crumbs; they go rancid.)

2. *Toasted Coconut, Sesame Seeds, Crushed Nuts, Oatmeal:* You can toast any of these by spreading them in a thin layer on a foil sheet in the grill pan, and grilling very gently until they colour. The pan must be shaken almost continuously to prevent them burning, but it is quicker and easier than toasting in the oven. Alternatively, toast the shreds, seeds or crushed food in a dry or very lightly greased frying pan.

3. Add *crushed or ground dried herbs* to any kind of crumbs for savoury toppings; use them discreetly for sweet toppings too. Try using whole dill or caraway seeds, or crushed allspice berries for a change.

4. *Dried lemon or orange rind* gives a tangy flavour to coatings for savoury and sweet dishes, and can be used in cakes and puddings if fresh rind is not available. To make it for storage, pare the thin yellow skin off the fruit with a potato peeler, dry it in the oven, then pulverize it in a blender or grind in a pepper mill. Store in a screw-topped jar for up to three weeks.

If you always pare a lemon or orange before squeezing it, you will soon accumulate a jarful of fragrant flavouring at no cost.

SWEET CRUMBLE TOPPING

For topping to cover two 7½-inch (17–18 cm) cakes, use:

> 3 oz (75 g) butter or margarine
> 6 oz (150 g) dried wholemeal breadcrumbs
> 2 oz (50 g) natural demerara sugar
> 1–2 teaspoons (1–2 × 5 ml spoons) ground cinnamon

Melt the fat in a large frying pan, put in the crumbs and turn them over with a spatula until light brown and slightly crisp. Mix in the sugar and cinnamon together, thoroughly. Cool on a plate, then store in a screw-topped jar in the refrigerator, for up to 3 weeks.

GRILLED COCONUT CRUMBLE TOPPING

For topping to cover one 13 × 9 inch (32 × 22 cm) slab cake, use:

> 2 oz (50 g) butter or margarine
> 4 oz (100 g) natural demerara or light muscovado sugar
> 3 oz (75 g) desiccated coconut
> 3 tablespoons (3 × 15 ml spoons) single or double cream

See that the top of the cake is flat and level. Wipe off any loose crumbs. Soften the butter or margarine, then work in all the other ingredients. Spread the topping all over the cake-top, preferably when still just warm from the oven. Grill gently for 2–3 minutes until the topping is bubbling and light gold.

TOASTED NUT BRITTLE COATING OR TOPPING (PRALINE)

You can store this coating in a screw-topped or other airtight glass jar just 'on the shelf', to use whenever you need it. If you pulverize it—very carefully to prevent it turning to paste—you can mix it into cakes, custards or ice creams to flavour them.

For storage or for enough coating to cover one 8-inch (20 cm) dessert or cake, or 4 individual desserts or ice creams, use:

> 2 oz (50 g) chopped almonds or hazelnuts
> 1 teaspoon (1 × 5 ml spoon) frying oil
> oil for greasing
> 2 oz (50 g) white (caster) sugar (see note)
> a 1-inch (2.5. cm) piece of vanilla pod if you wish
> 1 small blade mace if you wish (if using hazelnuts)
> 2 teaspoons (2 × 5 ml spoons) hot water

The nuts must be fairly finely and evenly chopped or some will grind down to paste before the rest are crushed.

Film the bottom of a small frying pan with frying oil, put it over low heat and add the nuts. Stir them until they are just golden. Tip them on to a sheet of paper at once.

Film a stone slab or heavy metal baking sheet with oil. Put the sugar in a small saucepan with the vanilla pod and mace if used, and the hot water. Heat to boiling point and cook gently for 3–4 minutes, stirring once or twice, until the sugar begins to turn golden. Stir in the nuts, by which time the sugar will all be golden. Immediately, spoon the mixture on to the slab or sheet, and remove the vanilla pod and mace. Leave the brittle until quite cold. Then crush it to a coarse crumbly powder. This is best done in a mortar with a heavy pestle—a nut or pepper mill, or an electric blender, may grind the nuts to a paste almost at once.

It is wisest to use white sugar because you can see instantly when it begins to turn golden. This is critical because it can turn treacly within a few seconds.

JAM GLAZE

Make enough jam glaze to store if you can. It is wasteful to make it each time you need it. Store it in a heatproof jar or pot, so that you can easily reheat it for use by standing the pot in a pan of simmering water.

LIGHT GLAZE

This glaze is suitable for painting on cakes, buns or biscuits before coating them with a loose covering such as crumbs, nuts or seeds.

> 1 lb (450 g) sieved apricot jam or redcurrant jelly
> 2 tablespoons (2 × 15 ml spoons) lemon juice
> 2 tablespoons (2 × 15 ml spoons) water

Put all the ingredients in a saucepan, and stir over a low heat until the jam or jelly dissolves. Bring to the boil, then simmer for 4 minutes or until the colour darkens slightly. Pour the glaze into a heated jar or pot with a screw-top lid, and cover at once with a disc of waxed paper to prevent a skin forming. Use warm; or cool completely, cover and store like jam. Reheat gently, if required, before use.

SETTING GLAZE

This is a stiffer glaze which will neither sink in nor be sticky when it cools. It is suitable for painting over cakes if you are not using a loose coating or icing. Use it as a shiny glaze on fruit flans and tartlets too.

> 12 oz (300 g) sieved apricot jam or redcurrant jelly
> 4 tablespoons (4 × 15 ml spoons) clear honey
> a few drops of lemon juice

Put all the ingredients in a saucepan and stir with a wooden spoon over medium heat until the jam or jelly dissolves and the mixture boils. Boil for 3 minutes or until the glaze makes a slightly sticky, thin coating on the spoon (about 225°F, 107°C). Take the pan off the heat at once, and spoon the glaze into a heated jar or pot with a screw-top lid. Use while still warm; or cool, then cover and store like jam. Reheat gently, if required, before use.

ORANGE SHRED TOPPING (Shredded orange rind in syrup)

For puddings, fruit tarts and other fruit desserts, and ice creams.

> oranges
> white granulated sugar
> ground cinnamon or crushed dried rosemary, if you wish

Use white sugar for this preserve because brown sugar or honey will dull its brilliance.

Pare the thin yellow outer skin off an orange with a potato peeler before you squeeze the orange or use the flesh. Snip the rind into matchstick shreds with scissors. Put a layer of the shreds in a small, flat-topped jar with a screw-on lid, adding a pinch of other flavouring if you wish. Sprinkle well with sugar, then add alternate extra layers of shreds and sugar until you have used your supply. You need not fill the jar. Close it and shake it vigorously, then stand it in a small saucer. After a few hours, turn the jar upside down in the saucer. Leave it for 24 hours, then turn it right way up. Continue doing this daily for a week, adding more shreds and sugar whenever you use an orange. The shreds will 'pack down' so there will always be room for more. They will also make a good deal of syrup, so keep the jar in the saucer in case any leaks out. After a week, all you need do is shake the jar from time to time. Take out a few shreds whenever you want a decorative topping for a pudding or dessert, and top up with new shreds when convenient.

This shredded orange rind topping keeps its fragrance and a brilliant colour for several weeks. It looks superb on top of a ginger or lemon steamed pudding, even better over caramelized oranges in ice cream.

The syrup is delicious too, especially as a sauce for vanilla ice cream.

HONEY ICING

For icing to cover the top and sides or 2 layers of one 7-inch (17.5 cm) cake, use:

> 1 egg white
> 2 oz (50 g) clear honey
> a pinch of salt
> ½ teaspoon (1 × 2.5 ml spoon) strained lemon juice

Put the egg white, honey and salt in the top of a double boiler over cold water. Place over medium heat, and beat or whisk with a rotary or electric beater, slowly, until the water is on the boil. Simmer, still beating, for 7–8 minutes or until the icing holds its shape when you lift the beater. Take off the heat, and continue beating until it is as firm as you want it.

Stuffings and Fillings

WHOLEMEAL HERB STUFFING (Basic breadcrumb stuffing)

You can vary this wholemeal breadcrumb stuffing in many ways; for instance, by adding chopped dried fruit or crushed (not ground) nuts. Try spicing it more strongly, say with a pinch of chilli powder or half a very finely chopped fresh hot chilli. Grated fresh ginger root with pinches of garam masala and ground coriander make it a good curry-flavoured filling for small turnovers.

For about 8 oz (200 g) basic stuffing, use:

> 2 oz (50 g) margarine
> 4 oz (100 g) soft wholemeal breadcrumbs
> 2 teaspoons (2 × 5 ml spoons) natural wheat bran
> 2 tablespoons (2 × 15 ml spoons) chopped parsley
> 1 teaspoon (1 × 5 ml spoon) chopped fresh thyme or ½ teaspoon (1 × 2.5 ml spoon) crushed dried thyme
> 2 teaspoons (2 × 5 ml spoons) grated onion
> grated rind of ½ lemon
> salt and pepper

Melt the fat and mix in the breadcrumbs and bran. Turn over until well coated. Take the pan off the heat, and mix in the herbs, onion, lemon rind and any fruit, nuts or extra seasoning you wish.

Use for filling a boned meat joint, a chicken, a vegetable or pancakes. The quantity given above will fill a boned leg of lamb, a 2¼-lb (1 kg) chicken or a medium marrow.

APRICOT STUFFING (Basic rice and fruit stuffing)

For about 1¼ lb (600–650 g) stuffing, use:

4 oz (100 g) dried apricots
1½ oz (35 g) brown rice
1 large cooking apple, about 9 oz (225 g)
juice and grated rind of ½ lemon
1 oz (25 g) pine-nut kernels
1 oz (25 g) margarine
salt and pepper
1 egg

Pour boiling water on the apricots, and let them steep until swollen and tender. Drain the liquid into a saucepan for cooking the rice. Add extra water if needed. Cook the rice as usual (page 81). Drain off any cooking liquid left.

Cut up the apricots roughly. Core and chop the apple, and mix it with the lemon juice and rind. Chop the nuts coarsely. Melt the margarine. Mix all the stuffing ingredients together, binding them thoroughly with the egg.

Use the mixture to stuff a small turkey, 2 small chickens, a large marrow or a small pumpkin.

BUCKWHEAT STUFFING (Basic grain stuffing)

Compared with some other grains and pulses, buckwheat is expensive and laborious to cook, but those who like its flavour soon become addicts.

For about 1¼ lb (600–650 g) stuffing, use:

½ pint (250 ml) water
salt
5 oz (125 g) roasted buckwheat (kasha)
1 medium onion
1 tablespoon (1 × 15 ml spoon) margarine
2 oz (50 g) seedless raisins
1 oz (25 g) chopped walnuts
pepper
1 tablespoon (1 × 15 ml spoon) chopped parsley
1 teaspoon (1 × 5 ml spoon) finely chopped fresh sage
   leaves

Bring the water to the boil in a large saucepan with a good sprinkling of salt. Tip in the buckwheat, and stir round once. Lower the heat, half cover the pan, and keep at a slow boil for about 20 minutes or until the grain is half-cooked and all the water has been absorbed. Add a very little more water while cooking if you must, to prevent it burning, but no more than you need. When ready, the buckwheat should be quite dry. While it cooks, chop the onion and fry it in the fat until soft.

Mix the onion, any remaining fat and all the other ingredients into the buckwheat when it is ready, and let it cool completely before using.

This quantity of stuffing should be enough to fill a small turkey. Certainly, if you pile it into two halves of a large marrow and then re-shape the marrow before baking it, you will have a passable imitation of a traditional Mock Goose. See Poor Man's Goose (page 77).

RED GLOW STUFFING (Basic soft vegetable stuffing)

For about 14 oz (400 g) stuffing, use:

    2 firm red tomatoes, about 4 oz (100 g) each
    1 sweet red pepper, about 4 oz (100 g)
    2 teaspoons (2 × 5 ml spoons) grated onion
    1 clove garlic
    2–3 oz (50–75 g) soft wholemeal breadcrumbs
    salt and pepper
    1 small egg if you wish

Quarter the tomatoes and remove any seeds from the pepper. Chop both together very finely, and mix with the onion. Crush and add the garlic. Mix in enough breadcrumbs to mop up the tomato juice, and season well. Mix in an egg if you wish, for a firmer stuffing.

Use for stuffing vegetables or as a filling for pancakes or wholemeal cannelloni. The vivid red, moist stuffing looks particularly good against the bright green peppers or the yellow of Corn-meal Pancakes (page 49).

The quantity above will fill 2 large sweet green peppers or 4–6 marrow rings.

MINCEMEAT 1975

This familiar Christmas treat and valued winter preserve has hardly changed in 200 years. We have reduced the quantity of meat and suet in the old recipe we used, that's all. Use to fill mince pies made from wholemeal shortcrust pastry; if you wish, add 1 egg to each 8 oz (200 g) mincemeat.

For about 5 lb (2.3 kg) mincemeat, use:

1½ lb (700 g) cooking apples
1 lb (450 g) currants
1 lb (450 g) seeded raisins
¾ lb (350 g) shredded suet
1 lb (450 g) Barbados or muscovado sugar
9 oz (225 g) lean beef mince
grated rind and juice of 2 small lemons
¼ teaspoon (½ × 2.5 ml spoon) ground mace
¼ teaspoon (½ × 2.5 ml spoon) ground cloves
2–3 drops cider vinegar to sharpen, if you wish
2½ fl oz (65 ml) brandy

Peel and core the apples. Mince the apples, dried fruit and suet together. Mix in all the other ingredients thoroughly. Store in airtight, vinegar-proof pots for at least a week before use. If stored for longer than 1 week, refrigerate. Use within 3 weeks.

Stocks and Savoury Sauces

VEGETABLE STOCK

For about 2 pints (1.1 litres) stock, use:

1 onion, about 4 oz (25 g)
2 leeks, about 4 oz (100 g) each
2 carrots, about 3 oz (75 g) each
¼ swede or ½ turnip, about 2 oz (50 g)
¼–½ head celery, about 5–6 oz (125–150 g)
1 large or 2 small tomatoes
a few coarse lettuce leaves
a few cabbage or spinach leaves

1 spiced herb bundle (see below) with 1 clove instead of
    allspice berries
2½ pints (1.4 litres) water
½ teaspoon (1 × 2.5 ml spoon) salt or as needed

Chop the sturdy vegetables and tomatoes, and cut the leaves
into wide strips. Put them with the spiced herb bundle into a
large pan, and add the water with salt to flavour. Heat to simmering point, and simmer for 1½ hours. Strain and add extra salt if
you wish. Pour the stock into heated bottles or a large jar, cover
and cool. Refrigerate as soon as it has cooled. Use within 36
hours, sooner if possible.

Note: Substitute 2 fl oz (50 ml) dry white wine for the same
quantity of water, if you wish.

AIDS TO MAKING SAUCES (and soups, stews and gravies)

SPICED HERB BUNDLE

This is our own version of a bouquet garni. Use a standard
bouquet garni in any of our recipes if you prefer.

    6 parsley stalks
    1 blade whole mace
    4–6 black peppercorns
    2 allspice berries if you wish
    4 sprigs fresh herb (thyme, marjoram, basil) if available, or 1
        tablespoon (1 × 15 ml spoon) of dried mixed herbs
    2 fresh bay leaves or 1 dried bay leaf

Put all the ingredients into a square of very thin cotton or muslin,
and tie opposite corners of the square over them so that they are
enclosed. Do not tie it too tightly, or the herbs will be packed too
closely to give up all their flavour.

DRIED MUSHROOM FLAVOURING (DUXELLES)

This semi-preserved mushroom flavouring is one of the most
useful things you can make as a kitchen standby, especially if you
live where field mushrooms grow. It flavours sauces, soups and
stuffings subtly and well when fresh mushrooms are expensive
or unobtainable.

For 4 oz (100 g), use:

8 oz (200 g) whole or tattered mushrooms, or mushroom stems
1 dessertspoon (1 × 10 ml spoon) butter or margarine
1 dessertspoon (1 × 10 ml spoon) tasteless vegetable oil (see note)
½ teaspoon (1 × 2.5 ml spoon) chopped parsley
2 tablespoons (2 × 15 ml spoons) chopped spring onion bulb or shallot
1 tablespoon (1 × 15 ml spoon) finely chopped large onion salt and pepper
1–2 fl oz (25–50 ml) Madeira or Marsala, if you wish

Put the mushrooms or stems in a clean cloth, wrap the cloth over them, and twist it to squeeze every possible scrap of moisture out of them.

Heat the fat and oil in a frying pan. Add the squeezed mushrooms, parsley, spring onion or shallot and chopped onion. Fry gently for 8–10 minutes until the mushrooms are dry, separate and brown. Season the duxelles, and add the wine for extra flavour if you wish, boiling it down quickly to nothing. Cool the duxelles in the pan, then refrigerate or freeze in any suitable covered container until you need your 'condiment'. Duxelles will keep in the refrigerator for at least 2 weeks.

Note: You can use any vegetable oil except olive or walnut oil.

BEURRE MANIÉ

The fat and flour paste called beurre manié is useful to keep in stock in the refrigerator, to save making a cooked fat and flour roux every time you need to thicken a sauce, soup or stew. For a pale smooth sauce, use 81% extraction flour. Mix together approximately equal weights of softened butter or hard block margarine and flour (or use a little more fat than flour). Blend them to a smooth paste.

Add beurre manié in flakes or small bits to any hot liquid, to thicken it. Do not let the liquid be on the boil, however, or the flour grains will burst before the fat melts, and will form lumps. Add the beurre manié to the liquid off the heat, and stir it until melted. Then return the liquid to the heat, and simmer it, stirring all round the pan, until it thickens. 4 oz (100 g) beurre manié make a thick coating sauce with 1 pint (500 ml) liquid. 3 oz (75 g) beurre manié make a fairly thick pouring sauce with 1 pint (500 ml) liquid.

You can store beurre manié in a covered carton in the refrigerator for about 2 weeks.

HOME-MADE MUSTARD

Your own home-made mustard can add a new piquant flavour to everyday foods, including sauces and salad dressing. Vary this one by substituting or adding other spices until you find the mix you like best. Once made, the mustard keeps for weeks in a covered carton in the refrigerator.

For about 8 oz (200 g) mustard, use:

  2 oz (50 g) mustard seeds
  about ¼ pint (125 ml) white wine vinegar or cider vinegar, to
    cover seeds
  4 tablespoons (4 × 15 ml spoons) dry white wine or dry still
    cider
  3 tablespoons (3 × 15 ml spoons) clear honey
  1 extra tablespoon (1 × 15 ml spoon) white wine vinegar or
    cider vinegar, or water (for milder flavour)
  ½ teaspoon (½ × 2.5 ml spoon) salt
  ¼ teaspoon (¼ × 2.5 ml spoon) ground allspice
  a good pinch of pepper

Grind the mustard seeds in a mortar, pepper mill or an electric blender before soaking them or they will make a very grainy paste.

Put the ground seeds in a bowl, and cover them with the ¼ pint (125 ml) vinegar. Leave them overnight; they will absorb all the vinegar.

Put the soaked seeds and all the other ingredients in a mortar or the goblet of an electric blender in the order above, and pound or process them until they are completely blended and more or less smooth. Taste, and adapt the flavouring if you wish. If the mustard is stiffer than you want it, add a little more wine or cider, or a little honey, depending on the mustard's flavour.

The mustard will be sharper if you use wine vinegar and wine than if you use cider.

VEGETABLE CREAM SAUCE (Basic recipe for thick vegetable sauce—hot or cold)

Try this unusual way of making a basic thick sauce. If you use a bland pulse, add a pinch of grated nutmeg or mixed spice and a sprinkling of chopped parsley to the sauce.

For about 8 fl oz (200 ml) sauce, use:

> about 2 fl oz (50 ml) strong vegetable stock (page 135)
> 5 oz (125 g) cooked firm white vegetable or pulse, such as cauliflower, young turnip, kohlrabi, celeriac or butter beans
> 2½–3 oz (65–75 g) cottage cheese or low-fat curd cheese
> salt and pepper if needed

Ideally, put all the ingredients in the goblet of an electric blender in the order above, and process them until they form a smooth thick cream. Without a blender, mince, pound and sieve the solid ingredients together, adding enough stock to moisten them as you do so.

These quantities make a thick coating sauce when made in a blender. For a thinner sauce, add more stock. Heat the sauce, if you wish, but do not let it boil.

TOMATO COCKTAIL SAUCE (Hot or cold)

Use fresh, home-bottled tomato juice if you make your own and (naturally) fresh lemon juice.

For about 1¼ pints (700–750 ml) sauce, use:

> 1¼ pints (750 ml) tomato juice
> 8 fl oz (200 ml) water
> 1 tablespoon (1 × 15 ml spoon) Barbados or similar brown sugar
> 4 whole cloves
> 1 teaspoon (1 × 5 ml spoon) Worcester sauce
> a pinch of cayenne pepper
> ¼ teaspoon (½ × 2.5 ml spoon) sea salt or ½ teaspoon (1 × 2.5 ml spoon) table salt
> 2–3 celery tops with leaves
> 1 dessertspoon (1 × 10 ml spoon) lemon juice

Put all the ingredients into a saucepan. Half cover it, and simmer gently for 20 minutes. Take off the heat and leave to stand until tepid. Stir any thick sauce from the sides of the pan, and strain the sauce into a bottle or jar with a well-fitting cork or lid. Cool completely, then refrigerate until wanted. Use, reheated or cold, within 3–4 days.

ITALIAN WALNUT SAUCE (Cold)

This beautifully creamy, cold purée or sauce is almost as famous as the Genoese Pesto, but it is wholly different in style. It can be served over any flat noodles or spaghetti. The hot pasta is simply tossed in melted butter before the sauce is mixed with it. The sauce is also often served over plain vegetables such as celery, kohlrabi or turnips.

For 4 helpings, use:

> 4–6 sprigs fresh marjoram or 6–8 sprigs fresh parsley
> 4 oz (100 g) shelled walnut pieces
> 4 fl oz (100 ml) double cream
> olive oil as needed
> salt and pepper

Pick the leaves off the marjoram or parsley stalks, and chop them very finely. Grind the nuts to a paste in an electric blender with the leaves, or mince them and then pound them in a mortar. (The paste need not be entirely smooth.) Mix in the cream slowly, blending it in thoroughly. You should get a fairly soft, pale green paste. Trickle in just enough oil to make the sauce a soft purée, and season.

Spoon the sauce over hot, well buttered noodles, spaghetti or vegetables when serving them. Fork it well in and eat the dish at once.

HOT YOGHURT SAUCE (Basic recipe—hot or cold)

This standard coating sauce lends itself to many different herbs and spices and can be served over fish, chicken or vegetables. The quantity here will coat a small cauliflower or marrow.

For about 6 fl oz (150 ml) sauce, use:

1 large egg
¼ pint (125 ml) natural yoghurt
1 teaspoon (1 × 5 ml spoon) home-made mustard
1 teaspoon (1 × 5 ml spoon) chopped fresh thyme or sage leaves
salt and pepper

Beat the egg in a saucepan until liquid. Mix in all the other ingredients and stir until they are well blended. Heat very gently without letting the mixture come near the boil, stirring all the time. Pour the sauce over the food to be coated as soon as it thickens, or serve it in a warmed sauce boat.

This sauce is also good cold.

Alternative

Use this version to make a Cheese Sauce of the standard creamy colour without white flour.

Stir in 1–1½ oz (25–35 g) grated mild Cheddar or Lancashire cheese as soon as the sauce thickens and is lifted off the heat. Stir round, to blend in and melt the cheese. Do not reheat.

TABLE OF FIBRE CONTENT OF COMMON FOODS

Food	Portion size (average)	Fibre (g per portion)
BREADS AND CEREALS		
bread: white	40 g (1 slice from medium-large cut loaf)	1.0
wholemeal	40 g (1 slice from large loaf)	3.4
Hovis	40 g (2 small slices)	1.9
Sunblest Hi-bran	40 g (2 small slices)	4.0
cornflakes	20 g (4 tablespoons)	2.2
Rice Krispies	20 g (4 tablespoons)	0.9
Puffed Wheat	20 g (4 tablespoons)	3.0
All Bran	40 g (4 tablespoons)	10.7
Weetabix	40 g (2)	5.0
bran	5 g (1 tablespoon)	2.2
VEGETABLES*		
beans: baked	100 g	7.3
runner	50 g	1.4
beetroot	40 g	1.0
broccoli-tops	50 g	2.0
Brussels sprouts	75 g	2.1
cabbage	75 g	2.0
carrots	75 g	2.3
cauliflower	75 g	1.3
celery (raw)	50 g	1.1
cucumber (raw)	10 g	0.04
leeks	75 g	2.9
lentils: split	50 g	1.85
lettuce (raw)	10 g	0.15
mushrooms (fried)	40 g	1.6

* Boiled unless otherwise stated.

Food	Portion size (average)	Fibre (g per portion)
onions	75 g	1.0
peas: fresh	50 g	2.6
frozen	50 g	6.0
chick-	50 g	2.6
potatoes	100 g	0.9
baked in jacket	100 g	2.0
frozen chips, fried	100 g	3.2
crisps	25 g	2.9
spinach	75 g	4.7
swede	50 g	1.4
tomato (raw)	50 g	0.75
canned, drained	75 g	0.7

FRUITS*

Food	Portion size (average)	Fibre (g per portion)
apple: eating—with skin	100 g (1 medium)	1.3
banana—with skin	100 g (1 medium)	2.0
cherries—with stones	75 g	1.5
currants: dried	25 g (1 tablespoon)	1.5
dates: dried—with stones	50 g	3.7
fruit salad (tinned)	75 g	0.8
gooseberries (stewed)	75 g	2.0
melon: honeydew— with skin	250 g	1.5
orange—with skin	200 g (1 large)	1.6
peach—with skin	100 g (1 medium)	1.0
pear—with skin	150 g (1 medium)	2.3
prunes (stewed)	75 g (5–6)	5.7
rhubarb (stewed)	100 g	2.2
strawberries	75 g	1.6

NUTS†

Food	Portion size (average)	Fibre (g per portion)
almonds	25 g (1 tablespoon)	3.6
Brazil nuts	25 g (1 tablespoon)	2.2
chestnuts	25 g (1 tablespoon)	1.7
hazelnuts	25 g (1 tablespoon)	1.5

* Raw unless otherwise stated.   † Weight without shell.

Food	Portion size (average)	Fibre (g per portion)
coconut (fresh)	25 g (1 tablespoon)	3.4
peanuts	25 g (1 tablespoon)	2.0
peanut butter (smooth)	20 g (1 dessertspoon)	1.5
walnuts	25 g (1 tablespoon)	1.3

Source: Based on figures in A. Paul and D. A. T. Southgate, *The Composition of Foods*, HMSO, 1978 (4th edition).

The foods listed below are good sources of the following nutrients

Protein
> meat, fish, milk, cheese, eggs
> pulses, e.g. lentils, dried peas, dried beans
> nuts

Iron
> offal, e.g. liver, kidneys
> red meat, e.g. beef
> pulses, especially baked beans
> cocoa powder, plain chocolate, black treacle, dried fruit, corned beef, Bovril

Vitamin B group
> wholemeal or wholewheat flour
> Brewers' yeast
> yeast extracts, e.g. Marmite
> pulses
> meat, including offal

Vitamin C
> citrus fruits
> strawberries
> blackcurrants
> potatoes

HELPFUL BOOKS TO READ

British Nutrition Foundation, *Why Additives?* (Forbes Publications, 1977)

Dixon, Pamela, *New Ways with Fresh Fruit and Vegetables* (Faber, 1973)

Eno, David, *The Little Brown Bean Book, The Little Brown Book of Greens, The Little Brown Rice Book* (Juniper Press, 1975–8)

Grant, Doris, *Your Daily Food* (Faber, 1973)

Hill, Ray, *Bran* (Thorsons Publishers Ltd, 1976)

Loewenfeld, Claire, *Everything You Should Know About Your Food* (Faber, 1978)

Stanway, Andrew, *Taking the Rough with the Smooth* (Pan Books Ltd, 1976)

INDEX